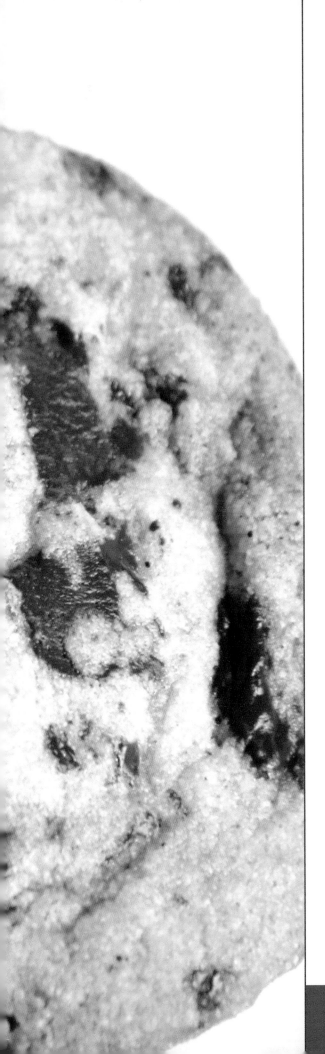

Thank You

I once heard someone say, "If you want to hear God laugh, tell him what you have planned!" That statement couldn't have been more true for the past few years of my life. I was totally a planner, and the more I tried to control how things happened, the more frustrated I got. My husband lost his job, my job as a rock-climbing guide didn't pay the bills and we struggled to start our family. All of these trials helped push me in the right direction to my nutrition business. Throughout this journey I have been able to befriend some amazing people that I need to thank.

Rebecca: I remember meeting you for the first time in BodyPump! Your talent as an artist is amazing! Thank you for all your support and encouragement. This book layout is all Rebecca!

Laura: You are my true "soulmate." I never thought I would meet a friend who I had so much in common with. I'll never forget walking with you while complaining that someone reserved the library book that I wasn't finished with yet and it was you! Thank you for the editing.

Jamie: I remember when you first approached me, "Maria, I love your book, but you need a new cover!" Your photography is indescribable! Thank you for the covers of all of my books! I also want to thank you for helping me start my blog; it helped me get up in the morning when I was going through the most difficult time in my life!

Craig: To my love and best friend. Without your technical skills, patience, editing, encouragement and APPETITE, none of this would have happened. SHMILY.

Table of Contents

Information and Recipes in Order of Sequence

Table of Contents

Information and Recipes in Order of Sequence

Introduction

You wouldn't put diesel in a gasoline engine and expect it to run…but that is what American's are guilty of doing to their bodies on a daily basis. We consistently fuel our bodies with processed, pre-packaged foods that evolutionary science has proven to make our bodies stop running efficiently; I was guilty of this also. I still remember sitting in the library at age 16. I tried on my friend Lisa's jacket. All of the sudden I heard a boy sing, "fat girl in a little coat." That started my wake up call. I wanted to be like Lisa; I hated always being the *fat friend* and never the *girlfriend*. I started skipping the afterschool trips to Tasty Treat for a gooey hot fudge sundae with the girls and replaced that with walking with my older sister. I also decided to create my own diet plan. I ate whatever I wanted for breakfast *and I mean anything*; my favorite was the leftover cinnamon rolls from the coffee shop I worked at. I ate a large salad for lunch with fat-free French dressing …yuck! Then diet coke for the rest of the day. Guess what? It worked, I lost weight…but I felt terrible.

I decided to study nutrition and exercise science in college. I met Craig (my husband) and fell in love. I started gaining the "love weight." I thought I would just kick my exercise into a higher gear; I started running and was up to 11 miles a day but I was still not losing any weight. I started running marathons and was considered a "Clydesdale" runner. My diet was filled with whole grain carbohydrates (for "carb-loading") and fat-free desserts.

Fat and frustrated, I finally decided to throw out the government recommendations of more "whole grains." I included more protein; especially for breakfast…skim milk in your Cheerio's doesn't count as a protein! After decades of being told by marketing geniuses that "fat free" was the way to lose weight, eating real fat was scary for me. Once I started adding fat to my diet, I slept deeper, felt calmer and better in that first week than I ever had. Now, I understand the biochemical reasons why restricting fat is not the answer. All my life I was taught that good tasting foods made you fat. It is almost too much to imagine that you can have total satiety while enjoying butter, avocados, grass-fed cheeses and meats, and even sugar-free cheesecake. But it has been over eight years and my body feels amazing and I never feel deprived. I traded in a lifetime of over exercising and fat restriction for a nutrient-dense, fat-filled diet and lost weight in the process.

Weight loss was a hard goal to achieve, but once I found the right foods and ditched the fake foods, it became easy. I learned the secrets of the hormone insulin and the lesser known hormone leptin, that by evolving toward a very low-glycemic, high-fat (not just high-protein) diet, I had re-sensitized my biochemistry to these essential hormones, which turn off severe food cravings. Best of all, my diet makeover required a lot less self-deprivation than what I was suffering from when I wasn't losing weight. The

nutrient-rich, relatively high-fat dietary approach I have developed for myself, with exotic, little-known replacements for typical high-glycemic starchy foods and sugar are what finally gave me total peace with food; something I never imagined possible. The weight came off, even more than my original goal. By the end of this book, I will show you these exotic tasty weight loss foods; such as almond flour for cookies and coconut flour for cakes. After all, we also need to enjoy the sweetness of life.

The love-hate relationship with food typically starts with innocent dieting and calorie counting, followed by out of control binging that causes dangerous extremes, such as skipping meals, obsessive-compulsive exercise, and purging. It is no wonder that food becomes the enemy; which is an unhappy state to be in. I help clients discover the beauty that nutrition can give us a life free from cravings and weight gain if we choose the right items.

Before my revelation of the biochemistry of food and our weight, I was so proud of my "perfect" diet of whole grains, fruits, and fat-free desserts, but I was still puzzled as to why I had uncontrollable cravings around food. By finding the correct supplements to change my biochemical imbalances, I started a high healthy-fat, grain-free, no starch diet; I finally found peace in my body. I didn't feel deprived or compelled to overeat.

The *'secret'* is to control leptin and insulin hormones. Any diet that stops blood sugar and insulin spikes also allows the cells to regain sensitivity to the noteworthy anti-aging, weight and hunger-regulating hormone called leptin. The hardest part is to get my clients to not be afraid of fat because it is almost impossible to obtain this effect without significant amounts of fat in the diet. High protein alone doesn't work because excess protein will also turn to sugar. Low fat, high protein diets will fail to keep your blood sugar from spiking, and will not allow your leptin hormone to increase. Ron Rosedale, MD, author of The Rosedale Diet and a pioneering scientist on the hormone leptin, states, "If you don't get enough fat, you will likely eat too much protein, which then turns to sugar."

I am writing this book to everyone who has been frustrated with the way they feel, inside and out. Maybe you look great, but nutrition isn't enhancing how you feel intrinsically. Nutrition is a huge part of how we feel and operate every day. I love feeling energetic and confident and I want you to also. I was miserable when I constantly deprived myself and felt guilty when I ate. I want you to also find peace and enjoyment with real food; which can turn into holistic peace in your everyday life.

Specific Ingredients:
Milk

The ingredients used in this cookbook are very specific. I have dissected all the macro and micro-nutrients to create recipes to keep our insulin levels low while keeping flavors high. For example, you will never see skim milk in my recipes for a variety of reasons, which you can read more on my chapter "Milk, Does it Really Do a 'Body Good'" in Secrets to a Healthy Metabolism.

UNSWEETENED ALMOND MILK - It is extremely low in sugar and carbohydrates, and it taste great. It only has 40 calories per cup versus 90 calories for skim milk.

COCONUT MILK - It is low in sugar and is healthy for SO many reasons...

1. DIABETICS: Improves insulin secretion and utilization of blood glucose. Helps relieve symptoms and reduce health risks associated with diabetes.

2. INTESTINAL DISORDERS: Helps relieve symptoms associated with gallbladder disease. Relieves symptoms associated with Crohn's disease, ulcerative colitis, and stomach ulcers. Improves digestion and bowel function. Relieves pain and irritation caused by hemorrhoids. Supports tissue healing and repair of the intestines. Improves digestion and absorption of other nutrients including vitamins, minerals, and amino acids. Reduces problems associated with malabsorption syndrome and cystic fibrosis.

3. ATHLETES: Provides ketones for a quick source energy. Boosts energy and endurance, enhancing physical and athletic performance. This also helps relieve symptoms that are associated with chronic fatigue syndrome.

4. IMMUNE SYSTEM: Kills viruses that cause influenza, herpes, measles, hepatitis C, SARS, AIDS, and other illnesses. It also kills bacteria that cause ulcers, throat infections, urinary tract infections, gum disease and cavities, pneumonia, and gonorrhea, and other diseases.

5. Kills fungi and yeasts that cause thrush, candida, ringworm, athlete's foot, diaper rash (infections).

6. Relieves stress on the pancreas and enzyme systems of the body. Reduces symptoms that are associated with pancreatitis.

7. OSTEOPOROSIS: Improves calcium and magnesium absorption and supports the development of strong bones and teeth.

8. HEART DISEASE: Reduces inflammation. It is heart healthy; improves cholesterol ratio reducing risk of heart disease. Protects arteries from injury that causes atherosclerosis and thus protects against heart disease.

9. AGING: Helps to protect the body from harmful free radicals that promote premature aging and degenerative disease. Does not deplete the body's antioxidant reserves like other oils do. Improves utilization of essential fatty acids and protects them from oxidation. Prevents wrinkles, sagging skin, and age spots.

10. KIDNEY STONES: Helps protect against kidney disease and bladder infections. Dissolves kidney stones.

11. WEIGHT LOSS: It is lower in calories than all other fats and it supports thyroid function. It promotes weight loss by increasing metabolic rate. Is utilized by the body to produce energy in preference to being stored as body fat like other dietary fats. Medium chained triglycerides produce ketones (energy) rather than being stored as fat.

12. SKIN DISORDERS: Applied topically helps to form a chemical barrier on the skin to ward of infection. Reduces symptoms associated with psoriasis, eczema, and dermatitis. Supports the natural chemical balance of the skin. Softens skin and helps relieve dryness and flaking. Promotes healthy looking hair and complexion. Provides protection from damaging effects of ultraviolet radiation from the sun. Helps control dandruff.

13. Does not form harmful by-products when heated to normal cooking temperature like other vegetable oils.

HEMP MILK - Hemp milk is growing in popularity because of its flavor and texture. It also has lots of nutrients including calcium, tons of vitamins, minerals, and essential omega-3 and -6 fatty acids.

Milk Substitutions (Per Cup)					
Item	Rating	Carbs	Sugars	Fiber	Calories
Skim Milk	Bad	13	13	0	91
Unsweetened Hemp Milk	OK	1	0	0	60
Unsweetened Almond Milk	Best	2	0	1	40
Unsweetened Coconut Milk	Best	1	0	0	50

NOTE: IF YOU HAVE A DAIRY ALLERGY, USE THIS GUIDE

1. Replace cream cheese, sour cream & cottage cheese with coconut cream

2. Replace butter with coconut oil

3. Replace heavy cream with coconut milk

Tip

All flours are not created equal. If you have coconut flour in the house and the recipe calls for almond flour, your finished product will not turn out. Baking with almond flour requires using more eggs to provide more structure. Use it in cakes, cookies, and other sweet baked goods. I buy mine at ....
http://store.honeyville grain.com/

Almond Flour

In my family we treat corn, carrots, potatoes and rice as starchy foods, as if they were sweets (starch and sugar = excess weight gain). They are all starchy carbohydrates as are the products made from them (chips, cereal, rice cakes and snacks). So we never use alternative flours made from corn, rice or potatoes. 4 grams of carbohydrates from sugar or starch becomes 1 teaspoon of sugar in our body! Baking with almond flour requires using more eggs to provide more structure. You can use it in cakes, cookies, and other sweet baked goods. I buy mine at http://store.honeyvillegrain.com.

It is important to use blanched almond flour. Most recipes will not work with unblanched; most almond meal (found at Trader Joe's) is made with unblanched almonds. Unblanched means the dark outside is on the almond; it creates a different texture in baking, which doesn't work as well to create soft baked goods. It makes a fine cookie, but it won't be as soft as a baked item made of 'white flour.' Here are some additional benefits of substituting almond flour for white flour:

1. DEPRESSION: Almonds contain tryptophan. This amino acid helps with serotonin production (the "feel good" chemical in the brain). When levels of serotonin fall, your body senses starvation. To protect itself, your body starts to crave carbohydrates. Serotonin levels fall after you go too long without eating, and that encourages your body to start filling itself (losing muscle).

2. HEART HEALTH/BLOOD PRESSURE/DIABETES (MAGNESIUM): What mineral is needed by every cell in the body, yet odds are you don't get enough of it? Hint: It's not calcium. Give up? It's magnesium. Magnesium deficiencies correlate to Alzheimer's and Parkinson's. Deficiencies also cause muscle spasms, pain, insomnia and fatigue. Magnesium assists in maintaining muscle mass, nerve function, a regular heartbeat, helps our immune system, and keeps bones strong. Diabetics benefit from magnesium as it helps regulate

blood sugar levels. In addition, magnesium normalizes blood pressure, and is known to be involved in energy metabolism and protein synthesis. There has been a lot of medical interest in using magnesium to avoid and manage disorders such as cardiovascular disease, diabetes, and hypertension. Almonds contain more magnesium than oatmeal or even spinach. It is found that magnesium deficiencies increase food cravings.

3. B-VITAMINS: These are our anti-stress vitamins. Vitamin B contents also promote healthy growth of hair as well as nails. I use almond oil on my skin everyday.

4. BONE HEALTH: 1 ounce (about 23 almonds) 20-25 almonds has more calcium than 1/4 cup of milk! A valuable snack in preventing osteoporosis. You will also build strong bones and teeth with the phosphorus in almonds.

5. CANCER: Almonds are the best whole food source of vitamin E, in the form of alpha-tocopherol, which helps prevent cancer. Using almond flour instead of white flour helps to starve the cancer from high levels of glucose on which it feeds upon.

6. FIBER: The high fiber content helps with weight loss by keeping us full and tapers blood sugar from spiking. The fiber also helps in proper digestion as well as enhancing energy levels.

7. PROTEIN: Almonds have protein. Using almond flour helps give us the protein we need to build proper bones (yes…bones need protein), helps us to focus, builds muscle and staves off sarcopenia. Sarcopenia is a natural process of losing 1% of you muscle per year starting at age 25! Yikes!

Coconut Flour

Coconut flour is unlike any, other consisting of 14% coconut oil and 58% dietary fiber! The remaining 28% consists of water, protein, and carbohydrate. It gives baked goods a rich, springy texture but needs a lot more liquid than other flours. For example you only need ½ cup coconut flour for about 6 eggs in a muffin recipe; therefore you end up with a high protein muffin rather than a high carb starch bomb. If you haven't tried coconut flour yet, here are some more excellent reasons to start:

1. LOW CARB and WEIGHT LOSS: Coconut Flour is ideal for baking. It has fewer digestible carbohydrates than other flours, and it even has fewer than many vegetables! Ideal for keeping blood sugar levels low, which helps weight loss. The high fiber content also promotes a feeling of fullness.

2. GLUTEN FREE: Coconut Flour is gluten-free and hypoallergenic. With as much protein as wheat flour, coconut flour has none of the specific protein in wheat called "gluten". This is an advantage for a growing percentage of the population who have a wheat allergy or sensitivity (many people have it without knowing it).

3. INDIGESTION: Indigestion is caused by excessive hydrochloric acid in the stomach. The acid, which sterilizes food and aids during the digestive process, is secreted by the stomach wall. Usually, the stomach wall is protected by a thick coating of mucus. Persistent high levels of acid cause this coating to break down, and the acid can attack the stomach wall, causing indigestion. Alcohol and acidic foods can further irritate the stomach wall. Coconut Flour consists of the highest percentage of dietary fiber (58%) found in any flour, which improves digestion.

4. CANDIDA, CRAVINGS and DEPRESSION: The intestines crave good bacteria which improve absorption of vitamins, decreases cravings and increases serotonin. Good bacteria flourish when we eat high-fiber quality food. Yeast causes an imbalance, letting bad bacteria in; they love sugar and starch. Yeast and bad bacteria damage the intestinal wall and produce toxic by-products which can be absorbed into the blood and sent throughout the body. This is how food allergies and leaky-gut syndrome begins.

5. PROTEIN: It is also high in protein which helps increase the Thermic Effect of Food, which increases metabolism. Protein also increases focus and mood.

6. REDUCES GALLSTONES: Gallstones form as a result of a gathering of cholesterol and salts from bile. Bile plays an important role in the absorption of fats from the intestinal tract because it makes fats soluble. Eating high fiber and low carb foods using coconut flour as well as LOTS OF WATER can decrease the chances of gallstones recurring. Galls are released by certain dietary fats.

7. IBS/CROHN'S/COLITUS: Irritable bowel syndrome (IBS) is a malfunction of the nerves in the wall of the bowel that make the bowel muscle contract. It can be connected to stress, vitamin deficiencies and low serotonin levels (depression). One treatment is to consume a high fiber diet; that in combination with coconut oil (a medium chained triglyceride) is VERY helpful for IBS.

8. HEART DISEASE/STROKE/BLOOD PRESSURE: Studies have proven that coconut fiber protects against heart attacks and strokes; it helps reduce cholesterol. Even modest increases in fiber intake can also significantly reduce blood pressure.

9. NO PHYTATES: Most fibrous foods such as seeds, wheats, and oats have phytic acid. This acid causes mineral deficiencies because it binds to minerals in the foods we consume (calcium, zinc and iron). Phytic acid pulls them out of the body resulting in mineral deficiencies. Coconut fiber does not contain phytic acid so it helps improve mineral status when you replace this for wheat flour in your baked goods.

10. HEMORRHOIDS: The high fiber content can help move things along. Just remember to consume extra water when you add in fiber or things can get worse!

11. DIABETICS: Coconut Flour consists of the highest percentage of dietary fiber found in any flour. Fiber helps moderate swings in blood sugar by slowing down the absorption of sugar into the blood stream. This helps keep blood sugar and insulin levels under control.

12. CANCER: Coconut flour is fermentable and produces high amounts of butyric acid which helps in stopping tumor formation. Studies have proven that butyric acid slows the growth of tumor cells and prompt all cells to develop properly. Coconut fiber also promotes good bacteria flourish which boosts our immune system.

The high fiber content acts like a broom, sweeping the intestinal contents through the digestive tract. Parasites, toxins, and carcinogens are swept along with the fiber. This prevents toxins that irritate intestinal tissues and cause cancer from getting lodged in the intestinal tract (decreases colon cancer). Since it is low carb, it also helps people maintain a low carb/sugar diet to stop feeding the cancer glucose which the cancer "feeds" upon.

NOTE: Not all coconut flours are created equal. Some brands have different baking properties.
I always use Coconut Secret Raw Coconut Flour.
You can find it here: http://astore.amazon.com/marisnutran05-20/detail/B003XB3NNE

PEANUT FLOUR - As long as you don't have candida, peanut flour is a flavorful ingredient. Peanut flour is a dry powder formed after the partial removal of oil from the nut. It is used to add flavor and protein to baked goods, snacks, as well as to sauces, marinades and dressings. While peanuts are about 25% protein, peanut flour is about 50% protein. That's because the process of removing fatty oil from roasted peanuts enriches the levels of the remaining peanut components. The resulting flour is naturally low in fat, high in protein and relatively low in carbohydrates. It is a great thickener for soups, a flavorful and aromatic ingredientfor breads and pastries, as well as a creative coating for meats, fish, and other dishes. Peanut flour is a good source of Vitamin E, Folate, Fiber, Niacin, Magnesium, and Phosphorus. Peanut flour is not self-rising and will need a rising agent added if called for in your recipe. When baking with peanut flour, you may want to add an extra egg or other moistening agent to prevent dryness.

HAZELNUT FLOUR - Using this for baked goods gives your dough a sweet nuttiness as well as fiber and iron. After first being diagnosed with a gluten allergy, you may feel tired; this is linked to an iron deficiency. I like to make my muffins with this. Nuts are considered a carbohydrate; however hazelnuts are very low in starch.

FLAXSEED - This seed has many health benefits such as high-quality protein, fiber, B and C vitamins, iron, and zinc, anti-cancer properties, omega-3 fatty acids, and many other benefits. To use as an egg substitute grind 2 tablespoons flaxseed and add 6 tablespoons boiling water. I have a chocolate flaxseed muffin in the recipe section that is a favorite of many clients.

PSYLLIUM HUSK - It is a powerful fiber that can be used in place of white flour in many baked goods. Some benefits include:

1. Maintains healthy cholesterol levels, including a proper balance of HDL and LDL cholesterol.
2. Decreases Constipation: Unlike stimulant laxatives, Psyllium husks are gentle and are not habit forming. Psyllium husks' bulking action makes elimination easier and more comfortable.
3. Reduces Toxins and Estrogen Dominance: Psyllium sweeps waste, excess estrogen and toxins more quickly out of the body, so toxins are not reabsorbed from the colon back into the bloodstream.
4. Reduces the risk of getting colon cancer and hemorrhoids, alleviates bladder and kidney problems, help lower blood glucose in diabetics, helps to make labor easier by dilating the cervix, and helps dieters lose more weight.

5. Natural Antibiotic: It is sold as a cough syrup in many parts of the world. In Argentina it is brewed and strained, then chilled and used to reduce inflammation. In India it is used to treat rheumatism and gout in a mixture of oil and vinegar. Old World remedies used psyllium seeds in a poultice to treat wounds and sores.

6. Gluten-Free: Psyllium husks do not contain any gluten so people who are gluten sensitive can use them.

Flour Substitutions (Per Cup)					
Item	Rating	Carbs	Sugars	Fiber	Calories
Rice Flour (Gluten-Free)	Bad	127	0.2	3.8	578
White Flour	Bad	100	0	4	496
Wheat Flour	Bad	87	0	14	407
Oat Flour	Bad	78	0	12	480
Almond Flour	Best	24	4	12	640
Peanut Flour	Best	21	4	9	196
Coconut Flour	Best	80	0	48	480
Flaxseed Meal	Best	32	0	32	480
Psyllium Husk	Best	80	0	72	280

The more sugar we eat, the more we crave it. If you start your day off with cereal and skim milk, you aren't going to be able to walk by the candy jar in your office at 2pm! Check out these to breakfast comparisons:

Option 1: 1 cup SMART START Cereal (1 cup skim milk and banana)
472 calories, 105 carbs, 4g fiber = 25.25 tsp of sugar in blood (IF you didn't add any sugar!)

Option 2: 2 eggs, with 2 cups of mushrooms, peppers, onions
190 calories, 9 carbs, 3 fiber = 1.5 tsp of sugar in blood

Option 3: My homemade donut made with coconut flour
217 calories, 7.4 carbs, 4.6g fiber = 0.7 tsp of sugar in blood!

To eat is a necessity; to eat 'healthy' is an art.

Sugar Alternatives

If you crave sweets while trying to conquer addictions to food, drugs or alcohol then the sweetness of these alternative sweeteners can help to fulfill these cravings in a healthy manner and not play havoc with weight and blood sugar. Here are the natural sweeteners I use and why.

STEVIA GLYCERITE - Stevia glycerite is a favorite of many people. It is an herb that has been used as a sweetener in South America for hundreds of years. One tip is to look for "stevia glycerite;" which has no bitter aftertaste as compared to plain "stevia. It is widely used all over the world. In Japan, it claims 58% of the sweetener market, and was used in Japanese Diet Coke until the company replaced it with aspartame to "standardize" worldwide.

> CALORIES = 0
> SWEETNESS = 300 times sweeter than sugar
> CONVERSION = 1 tsp stevia = 1 cup of sugar

WHY I USE IT: It is great for cooking, because it maintains flavor that many other sweeteners lose when heated, but it also needs an additional sweetener in most cases when making baked goods since it doesn't caramelize or create "bulk."

BENEFITS OF STEVIA

1. WEIGHT LOSS and DIABETICS: It does not affect blood sugar metabolism. This makes it a great tool in weight loss programs, but it also for diabetics. Stevia creates a hypoglycemic effect and increases glucose tolerance. It significantly decreases plasma glucose levels. In multiple human studies, blood sugar is reduced by 35% 6-8 hours after consumption of a hot water extract of the leaf.

2. BLOOD PRESSURE: Stevia extract is a vasodilator agent. Studies show that a mix of hot water and extract from the leaf lowers both systolic and diastolic blood pressure. Several studies demonstrated this hypotensive action (as well as a diuretic action).

3. ANTI-BACTERIAL/ANTI-YEAST: has anti-bacterial properties in that it helps to inhibit the growth and reproduction of harmful bacteria that lead to disease. It helps prevent dental cavities by inhibiting the bacteria Streptococcus mutans that stimulates plaque growth. It also has vasodilatory activity and is effective for various skin issues, such as acne, heat rash, and problems caused by insufficient blood circulation.

4. CANCER: It keeps your body in a ketogenic state so you can starve the cancer of sugar on which cancer feeds upon.

ERYTHRITOL - Erythritol is a naturally-derived sugar substitute that looks and tastes very much like sugar, yet has almost no calories. Erythritol has been used in Japan since 1990 in candies, chocolate, yogurt, fillings, jellies, jams, beverages, and as a sugar substitute. Erythritol, is considered a 'sugar alcohol' and is found naturally in small amounts in grapes, melons, mushrooms, and fermented foods such as wine, beer, cheese, and soy sauce. Erythritol is usually made from plant sugars. Sugar is mixed with water and then fermented with a natural culture into erythritol. It is then filtered, allowed to crystallize, and then dried. The finished product is white granules or powder that resembles sugar.

CALORIES = 0 to 0.2 calories/gram (95% fewer calories than sugar)
SWEETNESS = 70% as sweet as table sugar. Use cup for cup like sugar, but you need to add a tsp of stevia glycerite to add sweetness.

BENEFITS OF ERYTHRITOL

1. It has a crystallization property like sugar. This is why you can't just use stevia for baking.
2. WEIGHT LOSS and DIABETES: Erythritol does not affect blood glucose or insulin levels.
3. ORAL HEALTH: Erythritol isn't metabolized by oral bacteria which break down sugars and starches to produce acids, which means that it doesn't contribute to tooth decay. This is why excess carbohydrates and table sugar lead to tooth enamel loss and cavities formation.
4. CANDIDA: Erythritol is absorbed in the small intestines, which reduces fermentation and decreases the detrimental problems associated with Candida (yeast overgrowth in the body).
UNDESIRED PROPERTIES: It doesn't dissolve in foods (like salad dressings/caramel)

NAME BRANDS OF STEVIA-ERYTHRITOL BLENDS

1. TRUVIA: Coca-Cola brand. It is expensive and I don't enjoy opening a million little packets if the store doesn't carry the tubs. This is why I purchase erythritol and stevia glycerite separate.
2. ZSWEET: It comes in convenient large bags (as compared to the small tubs of Truvia). A lot of people prefer the taste of ZSweet over other non-caloric sweeteners.
3. ORGANIC ZERO: Is produced from Organic Sugar Cane Juice, which is naturally fermented and crystallized to create Organic Erythritol. Organic Zero is 70% as sweet as table sugar. You need to add 1 tsp of stevia to your baked goods when using Organic Zero.

Sugar Alternatives

XYLITOL - Xylitol occurs naturally in many fruits and vegetables and is even produced by the human body during normal metabolism. Manufacturers make it from plants such as birch and other hard wood trees and fibrous vegetation. Some people prefer the taste of xylitol. I only use it when I have to since it has a higher calorie content and causes an increase in insulin. Before I found JUST LIKE SUGAR, I used this for my caramel sauce.

CALORIES = 2.4 calories/gram; 1 tsp has 9.6 calories and 1 tsp of sugar has 15 calories calories
                    (40% fewer calories and 75% fewer carbs than table sugar)
SWEETNESS/CONVERSION = Same as table sugar. Use cup for cup.

BENEFITS OF XYLITOL

1. 40% fewer calories than sugar.

2. Researchers found that kids who consistently chewed Xylitol gum had 40% fewer ear infections than those who did not.

3. Pregnant women benefit from Xylitol to keep their teeth healthy especially during the third trimester, when teeth are especially soft.

4. Eating Xylitol gum or mints stimulates saliva flow. This will protect your teeth because it brings the PH levels close to neutral. (diet soda has a pH 2.2)

5. Reduces tooth decay: If you drink acidic sports drinks frequently, eat carbohydrates often and spend hours dehydrated and breathing through a dry acidic mouth, such as athletes and teenagers, these are risk factors for tooth decay. Xylitol can help.

6. Studies show that a consistent use of at least 6-8 grams of Xylitol daily can reduce cavities as much as 80%. If you already have gum disease or cavities, these problems can be reversed. Regular use of Xylitol can stop things from getting worse (along with a grain-free diet and increased consumption of fat soluble vitamins A, D, E and K).

UNDESIRED PROPERTIES: Xylitol has very few known side effects, although some people report diarrhea when adding xylitol into their diets. Note: Xylitol is fatal to animals...don't let your dog get a piece of sugar free gum!

NATURE'S HOLLOW PRODUCTS are made with xylitol: honey, pancake syrup, jelly, BBQ sauce, Ketchup

JUST LIKE SUGAR - Made from chicory root, calcium, vitamin C, natural flavor, orange peel.

CALORIES = 0

SWEETNESS = Same as table sugar. Use cup for cup.

Just Like Sugar has none of the strong aftertastes of stevia or artificial sweeteners. It also keeps ice cream soft, makes perfect caramel sauce, makes cookies soft on the inside and chewy on the outside, and it tastes great.

BENEFITS OF CHICORY ROOT

1. CHOLESTEROL: It decreases the levels of serum LDL cholesterol in the blood.

2. INFLAMMATION: It contains vitamin C, one of the most powerful antioxidants.

3. DIABETES: The inulin content is not digestible, so its lack of glucose can help promote optimal blood sugar levels while also increasing stool bulk and consistency.

4. CONSTIPATION: It provides soluble fiber, which improves digestion.

5. GALL BLADDER ISSUES: It builds your body's resistance to gallstones and liver stones. By increasing the flow of bile, it assists the body in digesting foods and liquids. The extra bile also helps break down fats in the body. Chicory root has a mild laxative effect, increases bile from the gallbladder, and decreases swelling.

6. URINARY INFECTIONS, KIDNEY STONES and GOUT: It has diuretic properties that provide protection for the urinary tract system and kidneys. Toxins are removed and the cleansing of the body is stimulated because of an increase in urine flow. It has been used to expel gravel, calcium deposits, and excess uric acid from the body, which helps to prevent gout and kidney stones.

7. WEIGHT LOSS: Chicory root benefits weight loss because of the effect it has on the digestive system. It is an excellent source of fructooligosaccharides which help promote the growth of beneficial bacteria in your digestive tract. It also increases the rate of the breakdown of fats. It also helps with weight loss because it helps keep insulin levels low while enjoying sweet foods.

8. NATURAL "Liver" CLEANSER: Chicory root also supports the body's detoxification system through the liver and kidneys, and is believed to help with calcium absorption. Chicory also helps prevent jaundice and an enlarged liver when mixed with water. Because of Chicory Root's potential for removing contaminants from the digestive system, the liver does not have to work as hard to filter out toxins that may have escaped into the bloodstream. It also acts as a gentle laxative and diuretic for removing excess water and toxins, and this can also reduce strain on the liver.

9. ANXIETY: It is a natural sedative and anti-inflammatory for the nervous system. If you have anxiety issues and still drink coffee, this sweetener can help.

10. INDIGESTION: It acts as an herbal antacid; the root neutralizes acid and corrects acid indigestion, heartburn, gastritis, vomiting, upset stomach. Because it stimulates bile production, this helps to speed up the digestive process after eating too much rich food.

11. SKIN: Used externally, the Chicory Root has healing properties for cuts, sunburn, swellings, hemorrhoids, and poison ivy. It reduces the inflammation of rheumatism and the pain of sore joints.

UNDESIRED PROPERTIES: It is expensive, but other than that it is perfect! NOTE: IT IS 96g fiber per cup so if you add it to liquid (such as melted butter) it will gel up.

ALLERGENS: If you are allergic to ragweed, you may be allergic to the Chicory Root.

CHOCOPERFECTION Chocolate Bars are sweetened with Chicory Root.

Glycemic Index of Sweeteners
Stevia Glycerite = 0
Erythritol = 0
Truvia/ZSWEET = 0
JUST LIKE SUGAR = 0
Xylitol = 7
Maple Syrup = 54
Honey = 62
Table Sugar = 68
Splenda = 80
High Fructose Corn Syrup = 87

WHERE TO FIND INGREDIENTS

Some of my specific ingredients are hard to find (or really expensive in grocery stores).
I created an online 'store' where you can find these ingredients at the best prices I have found.
For easy online shopping go to:
http://astore.amazon.com/marisnutran05-20

My recipes will call for erythritol and stevia glycerite. I use these separate to help keep my costs down. In any recipe you can use ZSweet, Truvia, Organic Zero, Xylitol or Just Like Sugar. In order to use a different product, use the same amount of sweetener for the amount of erythritol in the recipe and omit the stevia (except for Organic Zero, that is only erythritol and you will still need stevia for sweetness).

1 cup erythritol and 1 tsp stevia = 1 cup ZSweet

1 cup erythritol and 1 tsp stevia = 1 cup Truvia

1 cup erythritol and 1 tsp stevia = 1 cup Xylitol

1 cup erythritol and 1 tsp stevia = 1 cup Just Like Sugar

1 cup erythritol and 1 tsp stevia = 1 cup Organic Zero and 1 tsp stevia

NOTE: If a recipe calls for a specific sweetener, the final product will not be the same if you substitute a different sweetener, for example, ice cream will not be soft if you use all erythritol instead of Just Like Sugar.

Why Whey Protein

Tip

When buying a whey protein product, "Whey Protein Isolate" is the highest quality you can buy; which has at least 90% protein with only trace amounts o Also check the sugar count; some brands add way too much sugar to make whey taste like candy and get you hooked on their product…and that sugar isn't going to help our waist line!

Did you know that if you gain 10 pounds of muscle, you will burn an extra 3500 calories per week? To burn that many calories doing cardio, you would have to run for an hour each day of the week! To build 10 pounds of muscle, feed your body a high quality whey protein 1-3 times a day, and increase strength training. Whey protein is my favorite addition to my diet in the past few years.

TOP 10 REASONS TO CONSUME WHEY

1. Boost Immune System - Whey protein includes high levels of the amino acid cysteine, which produces glutathione, a potent antioxidant that maintains immune health. One of the first indications in patients with autoimmune diseases is a decrease in glutathione levels. Many studies have proven adding whey protein to patients with chronic fatigue syndrome, cancer, and HIV can greatly enhance their immune system. Scientists discovered that whey proteins stopped the growth of breast cancer cells in test tubes. It was also proven that when patients ingest at least 24 grams of whey a day they had a noteworthy reduction in the size of cancer tumors.

2. Enhance Infant Formula - Whey protein contains alpha-lactalbumin and is the main nutrient in human breast milk. This makes whey protein a very important nutrient to include in infant formulas and should be the first protein consumed by babies. Good news to mothers; the Journal of Pediatrics found that formulas with whey protein have been shown to help reduce the length of crying spells in babies with colic. Not all contain whey because it costs more.

3. Benefit Cardiovascular Health - Adding whey along with your doctor's prescription can be a great balance to help your heart. Clinical research discovered that whey protein reduces blood pressure in individuals who are borderline hypertensive.

4. Increase Lean Body Mass - Our muscles need branched chain amino acids (BCAAs) during long periods of exercise and added stress, which can

also have a negative effect on the immune system. Whey proteins are naturally high in BCAAs that are easy to digest. It immediately supplies the muscles with the high quality protein it is screaming for, which directly correlates to an increase in physical performance and enhanced body composition.

5. Contribute to a Positive Mood - Stress is a well-known cause of a decrease in serotonin levels in the brain, which can cause depression. Clinical studies found that including whey protein is helpful in enhancing moods and in boosting serotonin levels because it is high in tryptophan, a natural relaxant. Whey is great for people with high stress lifestyles and elevated cortisol hormones.

6. Superior Protein Source for Lactose, Casein or Gluten Free Diets - Whey protein isolate is the purest form and is over 90% protein. Whey protein isolate contains only trace amounts of lactose, therefore people with lactose allergies can safely enjoy whey. It is also a great protein source for people with Celiac disease who are on gluten or wheat protein-restricted diets.

7. An Appetite Suppressor - One of the nutrients in whey protein, glycomacropeptide, stimulates the release of cholecystokinin, which is an appetite suppressing hormone.

8. Stave off Osteoporosis - Osteoporosis affects over 25 million Americans. We have the highest rate of hip fractures, yet we have the highest intake of calcium in the world, next to Sweden. Studies show that low protein intake, including low levels of animal protein consumption, was directly related to increased levels of bone loss. Impact exercise, such as walking, and sufficient amounts of protein in the diet can enhance bone health and may help to reduce the frequency of osteoporosis.

9. Help Protect against Ulcers and Acid Reflux - Lactoferrin, a nutrient in whey protein, is a known inhibitor of many forms of bacteria that is responsible for digestive problems; such as gastritis and ulcers. In addition, recent animal studies show promising results that it also kills the bacteria responsible for acid reflux.

10. Aid Wound Healing - People who have burns or are recovering from surgery require additional protein in their diet. Exciting new studies indicate whey protein nutrients promote the growth of new body tissue.

Jay Robb is a superior weight loss brand that uses stevia to sweeten their whey; they also use whey sourced from grass fed cows not treated with rBGH (Growth Hormone). I'm not one to "drink" my calories...I like to eat! So, I use whey in many of my recipes.

Caramel Sauce

Baked Goods & Sweet Endings

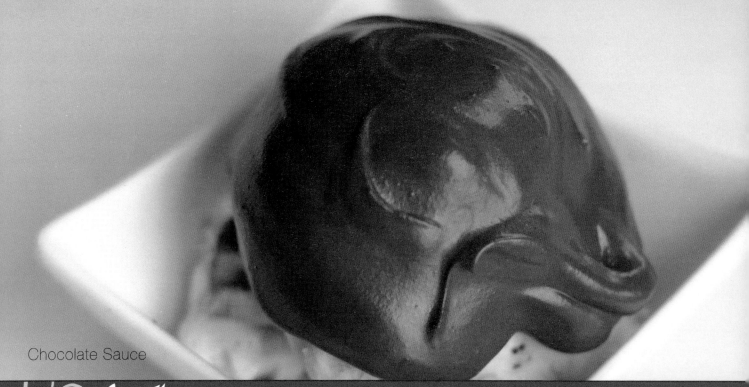

Chocolate Sauce

Many recipes throughout this cookbook use this caramel sauce. DAIRY ALLERGY: see pg. 9.

6 TBS butter
1 c. Just Like Sugar,® OR xylitol
1/2 c. heavy whipping cream

Just Like Sugar®: Before you begin, make sure you have everything ready to go - the cream and the butter should be next to the pan, ready to put in. Work fast or the sweetener will burn. Heat butter on high heat in a heavy-bottomed 2-quart (2 L) or 3-quart (3 L) saucepan. As soon as it comes to a boil, watch for specks of brown (this is brown butter....so good on veggies!). Immediately sprinkle in the Just Like Sugar® and the cream to the pan. Whisk until caramel sauce is smooth. Let cool in the pan for a couple minutes, and then pour into a glass mason jar and let sit to cool to room temperature. Store in the refrigerator up to 2 weeks.

Xylitol: Again have everything ready. Wear oven mitts; the caramelized sugar will be much hotter than boiling water. In a heavy-bottomed 2-quart (2 L) or 3-quart (3 L) saucepan, heat sweetener on moderately high heat. As it begins to melt, stir vigorously with a whisk or wooden spoon. As soon as it comes to a boil, stop stirring. You can swirl the pan a bit if you want, from this point on. As soon as all of the xylitol crystals have melted (the liquid should be dark amber in color), immediately add the butter to the pan. Whisk until the butter has melted. Once the butter has melted, take the pan off the heat. Count to three, then slowly add the cream to the pan and continue to whisk to incorporate. Note that when you add the butter and the cream, the mixture will foam up considerably. Whisk until caramel sauce is smooth. Let cool in the pan for a couple minutes, then pour into a glass mason jar and let sit to cool to room temperature. Store in the refrigerator for up to 2 weeks.

NUTRITIONAL COMPARISON (per 2 TBS)
Traditional Caramel Sauce = 130 calories, 12g fat, 0g protein, 24 carbs, 0g fiber
"Healthified" Just Like Sugar Caramel = 51 calories, 12g fat, 0g protein, 12 carbs, 12g fiber, (0 effective)
"Healthified" Xylitol Caramel = 60 calories, 12g fat, 0g protein, 1 carb, 0g fiber (1 effective)

Chocolate Sauce

2 TBS butter or
  coconut oil
1 oz unsweetened
  baking chocolate
10 TBS heavy cream
  or coconut milk
1/4 c. powdered erythritol
1 tsp stevia glycerite

Place the butter and chopped chocolate in a double boiler (or in a heat safe dish over a pot of boiling water). Stir well until just melted (don't burn the chocolate!), add in the cream, and sweetener. Stir until smooth and thick.

Makes 12 servings.
NUTRITIONAL COMPARISON (per serving)
Traditional Chocolate Sauce = 92 calories, 7.8g fat, 0.8g protein, 6 carbs, 0 fiber
"Healthified" Chocolate Sauce = 75 calories, 7.8g fat, 0.8g protein, 1 carb, 0 fiber

Control Blood Pressure

Are you on a high grain, low fat diet...like most Americans? Most people who are insulin resistant also have high blood pressure, and insulin resistance is directly caused by a high sugar, high grain (even "complex carbs") diet. So high blood pressure and uncontrolled blood sugar go hand in hand. As your insulin level increases, so does your blood pressure. Insulin stores magnesium, but if your insulin receptors are blunted and your cells grow resistant to insulin, you can't store magnesium so it passes out of your body through urination. Magnesium in your cells relaxes muscles. If your magnesium level is too low, your blood vessels will constrict rather than relax, which will raise your blood pressure and decrease your energy level. Most Americans are very deficient in Magnesium.

Insulin also affects your blood pressure by causing your body to retain sodium. Sodium retention causes fluid retention. Fluid retention in turn causes high blood pressure, and can lead to congestive heart failure. To enhance your heart health, the first thing ISN'T to count sodium (WELL, I would get rid of junky table salt and use a quality mineralized salt), it is to remove all grains and sugars, mainly fructose, from your diet until blood pressure and weight is under control. Eating sugar and grains (including ANY type of bread, pasta, corn, potatoes, or ANY type of rice) will cause your insulin levels, and your blood pressure to rise.

Fructose is a sugar that can only be metabolized by the liver, which breaks down into a variety of waste products that are unhealthy for your body, one of which is uric acid. Uric acid drives up your blood pressure by inhibiting the nitric oxide in your blood vessels. Nitric oxide helps your vessels maintain their elasticity, so nitric oxide suppression leads to increases in blood pressure. The average American now consumes 70 grams of fructose EVERY day!

STEPS FOR SUCCESS

Avoid foods that boost insulin levels. Even whole, organic grains will rapidly break down to sugars, so they too should be avoided. "Complex Carbs" are just glucose molecules hooked together in long chains.
1. SKIP THE:

      Breads.....try my **"Heathified" Breads, Waffles, Pancakes, Muffins and Bagels**

      Pasta.......try my **"Healthified" Pasta Dishes**

      Rice.........try my **"Healthified" Cauliflower Rice**

      Cereal......try my **"Healthified" "FAUX OATMEAL", Cream of Whey and Granola**

      Potatoes...try my **"Healthified" FAUX-TATOES!**

      Cookies...try my **"Healthified" Cookies**

2. INCREASE VITAMIN C: While vitamin C may be helpful, you'll also want to avoid eating too many fruits; the types and amounts being adjusted based on your nutritional type.

3. ADD GARLIC: One food that can be helpful for reducing your blood pressure is crushed, raw garlic.

4. OPTIMIZE VITAMIN D: Healthy vitamin D levels can have a powerful effect on normalizing your blood pressure. Low Vitamin D levels are associated with an increased risk for heart disease. Vitamin D has a positive impact on diabetes...it's all linked together.

5. BALANCE OMEGA 3 to OMEGA 6: Most Americans eating a standard American diet have a ratio of 25:1, which is super unbalanced. The ideal ratio of omega-6 to omega-3 fats is 1:1. To achieve this, lower the amount of vegetable oils in your diet, and consume high quality, animal-based source of omega-3s.

6. Take a Magnesium Supplement: Taking 400mg of Magnesium Glycinate right away in AM (blood pressure is highest in the morning) AND 400mg just before bed will help your blood vessels relax. Our food supply doesn't have the magnesium that it once did so a supplement is necessary.

FRENCH MACAROONS: Recipe on page 119.

Cavities and Bone Health

Did you know that you can reverse tooth decay and cavities? And re-grow bones? Many ground breaking studies and research have proven this. In one particular study published in the British Medical Journal and the British Dental journal, they divided 62 children with cavities into 3 diet groups for 6 months.

Group A ate their normal diet plus oatmeal (rich in phytic acid).

Group B ate their normal diet plus vitamin D.

Group C ate a grain-free diet and took vitamin D.

In group A, oatmeal prevented healing and encouraged new cavities, the phytic acid prevented mineral absorption. In group B, simply adding vitamin D to the diet healed many of the cavities and decreased the ability of more to form. The most shocking effect was group C, a grain-free diet plus vitamin D basically healed all the cavities and inhibited new cavities to form. Although group C contained no bread or other cereals, it included a moderate amount of sugar, for plenty of jam, potatoes and vegetables were eaten.

Dr. Weston A. Price also had success curing tooth decay using a similar diet. He fed underprivileged children one very nutritious meal a day and monitored their dental health. He also used high-vitamin pastured butter in conjunction with cod liver oil. We now know that the vitamin K2 in pastured butter is important for bone and tooth development and maintenance.

WHAT TO EAT:

1. No unfermented grains. Only true sourdough with NO lactic acid, but best = NO GRAINS.

2. QUALITY animal protein, eggs, grass-fed meat, organ meat, fish, bone broth, full-fat pastured dairy products (if tolerated).

3. Nuts; only if soaked overnight in warm water (to eliminate phytic acid).

4. LOTS of Vegetables!

5. Sunlight, cod liver oil and vitamin D3 supplements.

6. A good amount of pastured butter.

7. No food that comes from a box/plastic bag.

8. A limited quantity of low-sugar fruit (1/day or less).

9. No refined sweets.

Eating this way maximizes mineral absorption while also providing abundant fat-soluble vitamins essential for bones and teeth. Say goodbye to cavities and hello to healthy bones!

Cream of "Whey" Cereal

Ingredients:

2 c. warm almond milk

2 TBS coconut flour

2 TBS psyllium husks
   (or freshly ground flaxseeds)

4 TBS vanilla egg white/
   whey protein

1 tsp vanilla extract

1 drop stevia glycerite

1/2 tsp nutmeg

1/2 tsp cinnamon

OPTIONAL: add nuts,
   sunflower seeds or
   unsweetened coconut flakes.

Directions... Combine all the ingredients in a bowl.
Stir well and let sit for a few minutes or overnight until the
"cream of wheat" thickens (if you grind your flaxseed fresh, it
will thicken and it will have tons of Omega 3's). ENJOY!

Makes 2 serving.
NUTRITIONAL COMPARISON (per serving)

Traditional Wheat Cereal =
187 calories, 1.5g fat, 2.8g protein, 29 carbs, 2.8g fiber

"Healthified" Cream of Whey =
169 calories, 3.6g fat, 17g protein, 16 carbs, 13g fiber
                              (3 effective carbs)

Coconut Oil and Weight Loss

When you hear the words "butter" or "coconut oil" you have been trained to think "heart disease!" Well, I am here to tell you we have been replacing these natural good-mood fats with rancid vegetable oils (corn/canola/soybean) overloaded with omega 6 fats. Butter and coconut oil, actually protect the omega-3s in our brain. Outside of mother's milk, coconut oil is nature's richest source of medium chain triglycerides (MCT); they are extraordinary fats because they are not processed by your body in the same manner as long chain triglycerides.

Coconut oil increases thermogenesis, which increases metabolism and produces energy. The medium chain fats in coconut oil goes directly to the liver and are immediately converted to energy, we call these KETONES. It also increases metabolism because it is easily absorbed and produces organelles in our cells.

We have studied cows and other animals with different fats:
Feed animals vegetable oils = put on weight and produce fatty meat
If you feed them coconut oil = very lean

Normal fat metabolism depends on bile salts that have been released from your gallbladder before broken down in your digestive system. Coconut oil bypass bile metabolism and go directly to your liver where they are converted into ketones. The liver immediately releases KETONES into the bloodstream transported to the brain to be used as fuel.

BENEFITS OF KETONES:

KETONES - stable source of energy for the brain during periods of low blood sugar without the harmful neurological side effects associated with high blood sugar.
KETONES - preferred source of brain food in people affected by diabetes or any neurodegenerative condition such as Alzheimer's, ALS, Parkinson's, & Multiple Sclerosis. In these conditions, the brain can no longer use glucose for fuel so we need to use an alternative source...ketones!
KETONES - help heart patients recover from a heart attack and they can dramatically shrink cancerous tumors.

So let's use some flavorful coconut oil to help our brain and body!

Ingredients:

2 c. psyllium husks

2 c. chopped pecans

1/2 c. chopped walnuts

1/2 c. slivered almonds

1 c. sunflower seeds

1/2 c. sesame seeds

3/4 c. vanilla whey/
    egg white protein

1/2 c. erythritol

1 tsp stevia glycerite

1 tsp cinnamon

1/2 tsp Celtic sea salt

1/2 c. coconut oil or butter

1/3 c. Nature's Hollow
    Xylitol Honey/Syrup

Directions:

Preheat oven to 250 degrees F. In a large bowl, combine the psyllium husks, nuts, seeds, vanilla whey protein powder, erythritol, stevia, cinnamon, and salt. Melt the coconut oil, and stir it together with the syrup or honey. Pour over the dry mixture. Spray a big roasting pan with coconut oil spray, and turn the granola into it. Place in the oven, and let it bake for 40-50 minutes. Remove from oven and allow to cool, and store in an air tight container. Serve with unsweetened vanilla almond milk.

Makes 48 servings (1/4 cup serving).
NUTRITIONAL COMPARISON (1/4 cup serving)
BareNaked Granola = 130 calories, 5g fat, 4g protein, 22 carbs, 2g fiber
"Healthified" Granola = 110 calories, 8g fat, 5g protein, 9.7 carbs, 7.6g fiber

Trans-Fats: How They Are Made

Hydrogenation is the process that turns polyunsaturates, normally liquid at room temperature, into fats that are solid at room temperature; enter "I Can't Believe It's Not Butter"…I can! To produce them, food producers begin with the cheapest oils; soy, corn (I won't even get into Mansanto's GMO ROUND UP filled Corn and Soybeans!!!), safflower or canola, already rancid and full of free-radicals. Then they mix it with tiny metal particles, usually nickel oxide. The oil with its metal is then put into hydrogen gas in a high-temperature machine. Next, soap-like products and starch are added into the mixture to give it a better consistency; the oil is yet again subjected to high temperatures when it is cleaned by steaming. This removes its unpleasant odor. Margarine's natural color, an unappetizing grey, is removed by bleach. Dyes and strong flavors are then added to make it look like butter. The finished product is then squashed and packaged in blocks or tubs and sold as a "cholesterol-lowering" health food. Yikes! I'm sticking with yummy butter.

The extremely high temperatures, and the nickel that causes the hydrogen atoms to change position makes these items very harmful to our heart, cells and waist line! Before hydrogenation, pairs of hydrogen atoms occur together on the chain; this pattern is commonly found in nature. After hydrogenation, one hydrogen atom of the pair is moved to the other side so that the molecule straightens. This is called the trans formation, and rarely found in nature. These factory-made trans fats are toxins to the body, but sadly our digestive system does not identify them. Instead of being eliminated, trans fats are included into cells as if they were natural fats and our cells become partially hydrogenated! Once our cells become hydrogenated, our metabolism is slowed, not to mention the scary connection to cancer, digestive disorders and other diseases. It takes our body 9 months to metabolize trans-fast out!

Hydrogenated fats block uptake of essential fatty acids, causing harmful effects including cancer, atherosclerosis, diabetes, obesity, immune system dysfunction, birth defects, decreased visual acuity, sterility, low-birth-weight babies, and hardships with lactation. In 2000, scientific evidence emerged that the trans fats produced by hydrogenation affected fetal and infant growth. Yet, look at the false advertising, hydrogenated fats promote themselves as health foods. The attractiveness of partially hydrogenated margarine over butter represents a victory of advertising fraudulence over common sense. Professor Walter Willett, the principal investigator at Harvard called hydrogenation "the biggest food processing disaster in US history". In 2004 he told an interviewer that the advice to switch from butter to vegetable oils hydrogenated into margarine had turned out to be "a disastrous mistake".

These oils also produce Omega 6 in our body. Too much omega-6 causes inflammation, which is the beginning of all diseases (from cancer to obesity). Our blood vessels become damaged in a number of ways; through irritations caused by free radicals, or because they are structurally weak-and when this happens, the body's natural healing substance steps in to repair the damage; causing us to make more cholesterol.

Pancakes and Syrup

BUSY MOM TIP: Make the batter the day before and keep it in the fridge...it only takes a second to whip up a healthy, yummy breakfast.

Ingredients:

1/2 c. cottage cheese

2 eggs

1/2 c. vanilla egg white/ whey protein

2 TBS unsweetened almond milk

2 tsp aluminum free baking powder

SYRUP:

1 c. coconut milk (full fat)

1/4 c. vanilla whey/ egg white protein

1 tsp stevia glycerite

1 tsp vanilla or maple extract

Directions:

Place all ingredients in a food processor and blend until smooth. Let sit for 5 minutes (the baking powder will "fluff" up the batter). Heat a skillet and cook! I can take out this entire recipe without any guilt! But it serves 4. Just be careful with what you top them with! You can easily get up to 500 calories and a sugar coma with maple syrup. (Dairy allergy: see pg. 9)

SYRUP: Slowly sprinkle in the protein powder to the coconut milk (if you dollop the tsp in, it will thicken into a clump). Add in the sweetener and extract. Let thicken for 5 minutes. Enjoy.

Makes 4 servings.
NUTRITIONAL COMPARISON (per serving)
Aunt Jemima = 160 calories, 2.5g fat, 4g protein, 31 carbs, 1g fiber
"Healthified" Pancakes = 90 calories, 2g fat, 13g protein, 1.75 carbs, trace fiber
1/4 cup Aunt Jamima Syrup = 220 calories, 0g fat, 0g protein, 52 carbs, 0g fiber
1/4 cup "Healthified" Syrup = 140 calories, 14g fat, 5g protein, 3.4 carbs, 1.3 g fiber

Coconut Oil

A shocking study followed the effects of what happens to our body when we consume coconut oil vs soybean oil. They studied this on 40 obese women, age 20-40. The women consumed 2 tablespoons of either soybean or coconut oil every day while following a low-calorie diet and walking 50 minutes/day. The results will have you revamping your pantry and tossing your soybean oil filled Kraft salad dressing!

Now that consumers are getting savvy to the "partially hydrogenated" word on labels, manufacturers began switching over to a 'low linolenic soybeans.' This oil does not require hydrogenation, a process that increases shelf life and flavor stability, but also creates trans-fat. BUT do not be fooled, because these so-called "healthier" vegetable oils are still a terrible choice, as they create a disastrous imbalance of omega-6/omega-3 ratio that controls many delicate biochemical pathways, resulting in accelerating many chronic degenerative diseases.

Besides all this, soy, corn, and canola oils are made from genetically engineered seeds created to withstand otherwise lethal doses of Monsanto's Roundup weed killer, which is yet another reason to steer clear of these harmful vegetable oils. Coconut Oil, on the other hand, has many health benefits.

1. HEART HEALTH: Pacific Island populations who get 40-60 % of their diet from fully saturated coconut oil have all shown nearly non-existent rates of cardiovascular disease. It's been clearly established for over 80 years now that suppression of the thyroid raises serum cholesterol, while restoring the thyroid hormone brings cholesterol down to normal.

2. DIGESTIVE HEALTH (Babies-Elderly): Coconut oil is great for pregnant women, nursing moms, the elderly, those concerned about digestive health. One of the explanations for its broad health applications is because it's rich in lauric acid, which converts in your body to monolaurin – a compound also found in breast milk that strengthens a baby's immunity.

3. IMMUNE HEALTH: Its medium chain fatty acids, or triglycerides (MCT's), also impart a number of health benefits, including raising your body's metabolism and fighting off pathogens such as viruses, bacteria and fungi. Capric acid, another coconut fatty acid present in smaller amounts, is another antimicrobial component.

4. WEIGHT LOSS: Coconut oil is also excellent for your thyroid.

5. BRAIN HEALTH: A very exciting discovery is that coconut oil may even serve as a natural treatment for Alzheimer's disease, as MCT's are also a primary source of ketone bodies, which act as an alternate source of brain fuel because the brain can no longer use glucose for fuel.

mE
Maria Emmerich

Protein Waffles

Ingredients:

1 c. almond flour

1 c. vanilla egg white/
   whey protein

1/2 tsp Celtic sea salt

1 TBS aluminum free
   baking powder

1 c. vanilla almond milk

2 eggs

4 TBS butter or
   coconut oil, melted

Directions:

Preheat waffle iron to high. Combine the dry ingredients in a bowl. Combine the wet ingredients in another bowl. Slowly add the wet ingredients into the dry. Let sit for 5 minutes. Bake according to your waffle iron directions (I spray my waffle iron with Coconut oil spray). Enjoy!

Makes 8 servings.
NUTRITIONAL COMPARISON (per serving)
Traditional Waffle = 247 calories, 13g fat, 2g protein, 27 carbs, 0.7g fiber
"Healthified" Waffle = 182 calories, 14g fat, 14g protein, 3.5 carbs, 1.5g fiber

BUSY FAMILY TIP: Make a triple batch of these and keep in your freezer for an easy breakfast. Just pop one in the toaster like you would the chemical-filled Eggo Waffle.

Cinnamon Coffee Cake

Ingredients:

CAKE:

2 c. blanched almond flour

1 TBS baking powder

1 tsp ground cinnamon

3/4 tsp Celtic sea salt

2/3 c. butter or coconut oil

1 1/3 c. erythritol

1 tsp stevia glycerite

1 1/2 tsp vanilla extract

3 eggs

2/3 c. unsweetened almond milk

CINNAMON SYRUP:

1/2 c. erythritol

1 tsp stevia glycerite

6 tbsp butter or coconut oil

1/3 c. water

1 tsp vanilla extract

3/4 tsp ground cinnamon

CREAM CHEESE LAYER:

8 oz cream cheese, softened

1/4 c. unsweetened vanilla almond milk

1/2 tsp Stevia glycerite (or to taste)

Directions . . . CAKE: Preheat oven to 350 degrees F (175 degrees C). Grease a 9 inch pan. Stir together the almond flour, baking powder, 1 teaspoon ground cinnamon and salt; set aside. In a large bowl, beat butter, 1 1/3 cups erythritol, stevia, and 1 1/2 teaspoon vanilla until light and fluffy. Add eggs one at a time, beating for at least 1 minute after each egg. Beat in the almond flour mixture alternately with the milk. Pour batter into prepared pan. Bake in the preheated oven for 40 to 45 minutes, or until a toothpick inserted into the center of the cake comes out clean. Let cool in pan for 10 minutes, then turn out onto a wire rack. Remove cake from pan while it is still warm, and poke holes around the top of the cake with a fork. Pour the warm cinnamon syrup (recipe follows) into the holes and onto the top and sides of the cake.

CINNAMON SYRUP: In a saucepan, combine 1/2 cup erythritol, 1 teaspoon stevia, butter, water, 1 teaspoon vanilla and 3/4 teaspoons ground cinnamon. Heat and stir until butter melts. Pour onto warm cake.

CREAM CHEESE FILLING: beat cream cheese with 1/4 cup vanilla almond milk and stevia (to taste). You can make this ahead of time and store in the fridge (it will get thicker overnight). Dollop a tablespoon or two on top of cake. (Dairy allergy: see pg. 9)

Makes 14 servings.
NUTRITIONAL COMPARISON (per serving)
Traditional Cinnamon Cake = 391 calories, 20g fat, 3.6g protein, 45 carbs, 1g fiber
"Healthified" Cinnamon Cake = 293 calories, 27g fat, 6.1g protein, 6 carbs, 3g fiber

CINNAMON FACTS

1. Antifungal, antibacterial and antiparasitic - Cinnamon has been found to be effective in fighting vaginal yeast infections, oral yeast infections, stomach ulcers and head lice.
2. Anti-inflammatory - Many of us eat lots of fried, fatty and processed foods, and these foods cause inflammation of our internal tissues and organs, and this inflammation has been linked to one of the most life-threatening diseases of our time – heart disease.
3. Helps control blood sugar levels, and can significantly lower LDL "bad" cholesterol, total cholesterol and triglycerides (fatty acids in the blood). A now almost famous study, was conducted by researchers from the US Department of Agriculture (USDA) in 2003 that showed that people who had Type II diabetes, who ate 1 gram of cinnamon each day over a period of 40 days, experienced a significant decrease in their blood sugar levels, LDL cholesterol, total cholesterol and triglycerides.
4. Excellent source of manganese, dietary fiber, iron and calcium. The combination of calcium and fiber can help to remove bile, which prevents damage to colon cells, which helps prevent colon cancer. Fiber also can help with the relief of constipation and irritable bowel syndrome.

0

Gingerbread Donuts

Ingredients:

1/2 c. Just Like Brown Sugar

3/4 c. coconut oil or butter

1/2 c. unsweetened
   almond milk

4 eggs

1 tsp vanilla extract

1 tsp ground cinnamon

1/2 tsp ground ginger

1/4 tsp ground cloves

1/4 tsp ground allspice

1/2 c. blanched almond flour

1/2 c. coconut flour

1 tsp baking soda

BROWN BUTTER SAUCE:

1 c. butter

1 c. Just Like Sugar

1/2 c. unsweetened
   almond milk

2 TBS vanilla extract

Directions: Preheat oven to 350ºF. In a large bowl, stir the butter and Just Like Brown Sugar together. Stir in the almond milk, eggs, vanilla, and spices. Sift in the almond, coconut flour and baking soda. Mix into the butter mixture until well combined. Taste the dough and add more Just Like Sugar if desired. Grease a mini donut pan with coconut oil spray. Bake for 15 minutes or until a toothpick comes out clean. Serve with Brown Butter Sauce.

BROWN BUTTER SAUCE: To make the sauce, heat the butter in a heavy saucepan over high heat until the butter sizzles and turns brown (not black). Slowly sift in the Just Like Sugar. Stir well. Add in the almond milk and vanilla. Serve warm with the donuts. (Dairy allergy: see pg. 9)

Makes 16 servings.
NUTRITIONAL COMPARISON (per serving)

Traditional Mini Donuts =
369 calories, 20g fat, 1g protein, 27 carbs, 0g fiber

"Healthified" Mini Donuts =
249 calories, 25g fat, 3g protein, 6.4 carbs, 4.9g fiber (1.5 effective carbs)

Jiff Omega Peanut Butter Ingredients:

[Roasted Peanuts, Sugar, Contains 2% Or Less Of: Molasses, Fully Hydrogenated Vegetable Oils (Rapeseed And Soybean), Mono And Diglycerides, Salt], Anchovy* And Sardine Oil*,Tilapia Gelatin, Tocopherols And Citric Acid (Antioxidants). *A Tasteless, Odorless Source Of Omega-3 Dha And Epa.

Jiff Omega 3 Facts

What peanut butter do you use? I hope not Jiff "Omega 3!" The word hydrogenated oils = TRANS-FAT. There are many reasons why this word is so terrible for us!

1. DEPRESSION: Trans fats can lead to chronic inflammation which blocks the body's ability to produce mood-building neurotransmitter serotonin.

2. INCREASED APPETITE: Trans fats can lead to chronic inflammation which inhibits the body's ability to create appetite-controlling neurotransmitter dopamine and serotonin. Read more in Secrets to Controlling Your Weight Cravings and Mood.

3. WEIGHT GAIN: Trans fat slows the ability of muscle cells to use glucose as an energy source. When muscle cells can't use glucose, it stays in the blood and insulin levels severely increase. Excess insulin = fat storage.

4. ALZHEIMER'S: Patient's with Alzheimer's have brain cells that can no longer use glucose for energy (which is why I have my patients use coconut oil/ketones for a brain boosting energy source). One reason that this occurs is over time trans-fats inhibit the brain cells to metabolize glucose.

5. DECREASE IMMUNE SYSTEM and INCREASE CANCER: Trans-fats weaken the immune system by reducing the body's ability to fight viruses.

6. HEART DISEASE: Unlike healthy saturated fats that make up 50% of the cell membranes which create our cells necessary stiffness and integrity, trans-fats increase risks of heart disease. These factory-made trans fats are toxins to the body, but sadly our digestive system does not identify them as such. Instead of being eliminated, trans fats are included into cells as if they were natural fats and our cells become partially hydrogenated! It takes 9 months to detox trans-fats from our body.

7. OMEGA 6 OVERLOAD: Altered partially hydrogenated fats actually block use of essential fatty acids, causing many harmful effects including cancer, atherosclerosis, diabetes, obesity, immune system dysfunction, birth defects, decreased visual acuity, sterility, low-birth-weight babies, and hardships with lactation. So when you make these tasty treats, always use natural peanut butter with the ingredients: Peanuts and Salt! NOTE: If there is severe yeast overgrowth (candida), killing the yeast is essential to help restore good bacteria and therefore staying away from peanuts would be important at that time.

Maria Emmerich

Peanut Butter Donut

Ingredients:

1/2 c. coconut oil or butter
1/2 c. Just Like Sugar
   (or erythritol)
1 tsp stevia glycerite
3 eggs, beaten
1/2 c. natural peanut butter
3/4 c. sour cream
1 tsp vanilla extract
2 c. peanut flour
1 tsp baking powder
1 tsp baking soda
1/2 tsp Celtic sea salt

CHOCOLATE SAUCE:
See page 25.

Directions:

Preheat oven to 350 degrees F. Cream butter and sweetener. Beat eggs in well. Mix in peanut butter, sour cream, and vanilla. Combine peanut flour, baking powder, soda and salt together and add to creamed mixture. Spoon mixture into greased mini donut pan. Place in oven for 10-12 minutes. Test with a toothpick for doneness. Serve with chocolate dipping sauce.
(Dairy allergy: see pg. 9)

Makes 42 mini donuts, 12 servings.
NUTRITIONAL COMPARISON (per 1 serving)
Traditional Donuts = 396 calories, 18g fat, 1g protein, 49.5 carbs, 2.5g fiber
"Healthified" Donuts = 224 calories, 18g fat, 10.4g protein, 10 carbs, 7g fiber
(3 effective carbs)

mE
Maria Emmerich

Cinnamon Roll

Ingredients:

1/2 c. butter or
    coconut oil, softened

3/4 c. erythritol

1 tsp stevia glycerite

3 eggs

1/2 c. coconut flour

1/2 c. almond flour

1/2 tsp Celtic sea salt

1/2 tsp baking powder

1 tsp vanilla extract

CINNAMON FILLING:

3 TBS butter, softened

2 TBS cinnamon

3 TBS erythritol

1/4 tsp stevia glycerite

FROSTING:

6 TBS cream cheese,
    softened

3 TBS butter, softened

2 TBS erythritol

1/4 tsp stevia glycerite

3 TBS unsweetened
    almond milk

Directions . . .

Preheat the oven to 325 degrees F. In a medium bowl, cream the butter and the sweetener until very smooth. Add in the eggs. In another bowl mix together the coconut flour, almond flour, salt and baking powder. Slowly add the dry ingredients into the wet, then add in the vanilla. Stir until a thick dough forms. Place a sheet of parchment on counter, then spray with coconut oil spray. Place dough on greased parchment, push the dough down a bit, and spray with another layer of coconut oil. Top with another sheet of parchment. Roll the dough out with a rolling pin until it is a long rectangle shape (9x12) or so and 1/4 inch thick. Then remove the top layer of parchment.

CINNAMON FILLING: Mix all ingredients together and spread evenly over the dough...make sure the top layer of parchment is off :) Roll up dough using the edge of the plastic to make a tight log. Cut into 1 1/2 inch pieces. Place the rolls into a greased muffin tin or onto a pan right next to each other (so they hold each other up). Bake for 20-25 minutes or until baked through (insert a toothpick to check doneness....the toothpick should come out clean).

FROSTING: Place all ingredients into a medium sized bowl and combine until smooth. Store in fridge (it will thicken overnight). Spread over cinnamon rolls.

Makes 8 servings.
NUTRITIONAL COMPARISON (per roll)
"Cinnabon" Roll = 730 calories, 24g fat, 1g protein, 114 carbs, trace fiber
"Healthified" Roll = 257 calories, 23g fat, 4g protein, 6.9 carbs, 4.2g fiber

DAIRY FREE OPTION: Use coconut oil in place of butter and use coconut cream in place of cream cheese.

Benefits of Cholesterol

1. Cholesterol, along with saturated fats, gives our cells required stiffness and stability. When the diet contains an excess of polyunsaturated fats (vegetable oils or omega-6), instead of saturated fats in the cell membrane, the cell walls become flabby. If this happens, cholesterol from the blood drives into the tissues to give them structural integrity. This is why serum cholesterol levels may go down temporarily when we replace saturated fats with polyunsaturated fats in the diet.

2. Cholesterol is vital for production and function of serotonin receptors in the brain. Serotonin is the body's "feel-good" chemical. Low cholesterol levels have been linked to depression and aggression. Anti-depressants often don't work for patients that are on vegetarian diets.

3. Mother's milk is VERY high in cholesterol and has an important enzyme that assists the baby in using this nutrient. Babies and children need foods high in cholesterol to guarantee proper development of the brain and nervous system (BUT we also need these as adults!!!)

4. Cholesterol acts as a precursor to important hormones that help us deal with stress and protect the body against cancer and heart disease. It is also important to our sex hormones like androgen, testosterone, estrogen and progesterone. Which is why women trying to get pregnant have more success on a high saturated fat diet!

5. Cholesterol is necessary for us to use vitamin D; which is an essential fat-soluble vitamin needed for healthy bones and nervous system, insulin production, reproduction and immune system function, proper growth, mineral metabolism, and muscle tone. So why do they fortify SKIM MILK with Vitamin D??? What a waste of money!

6. Bile is vital for digestion and assimilation of fats in the diet; which is made from cholesterol.

7. Cholesterol performs as an antioxidant; which is why cholesterol levels go up with age. It protects against free radical damage that leads to heart disease and cancer.

8. Dietary cholesterol helps maintain the health of the intestinal wall. People on low-cholesterol vegetarian diets often develop leaky gut syndrome and other intestinal disorders.

Cholesterol can become damaged by exposure to heat and oxygen. This oxidized cholesterol tends to promote damage to the arterial cells and cause buildup of plaque in the arteries. Damaged cholesterol is found in powdered milk; which is added to reduced-fat milks to give them body. That is why I NEVER suggest drinking skim milk! It is also found in powdered eggs and in meats that have been heated to high temperatures in frying and other high-temperature processes. So fast food items come into play here. Hypothyroidism can result in high cholesterol levels. When thyroid function is poor, usually due to a diet low in usable iodine, fat-soluble vitamins and high in sugar, the blood gets filled with cholesterol as a protective mechanism, providing a large amount of minerals needed to heal tissues. Hypothyroid individuals are particularly susceptible to infections, heart disease and cancer.

Peanut Butter Biscotti

Ingredients:

1/3 c. butter
   or coconut oil

1/2 c. erythritol

1/2 tsp stevia glycerite

2 eggs

1 tsp vanilla extract

1 3/4 c. peanut flour

2 tsp baking powder

1/2 c. chopped
   ChocoPerfection Bar

1 egg yolk, beaten

1 TBS water

Directions:

Preheat oven to 375 degrees F (190 degrees C). Grease baking sheets, or line with parchment paper. In a large bowl, cream together the butter and sweetener until smooth. Beat in the eggs one at a time, then stir in the vanilla. Combine the peanut flour and baking powder; stir into the creamed mixture until well blended. Dough will be stiff, so mix in the last bit by hand. Mix in the chocolate chips and walnuts (if desired). Divide dough into two equal parts. Shape into 9x2x1 inch loaves. Place onto baking sheet 4 inches apart. Brush with mixture of water and yolk. Bake for 20 to 25 minutes in the preheated oven, or until firm. Cool on baking sheet for 30 minutes. Using a serrated knife, slice the loaves diagonally into 1 inch slices. Return the slices to the baking sheet, placing them on their sides. Bake for 10 to 15 minutes on each side, or until dry. Cool completely and store in an airtight container.

Makes 12 servings.

NUTRITIONAL COMPARISON:
Using white flour & sugar = 187 calories, 8.5g fat, 3g protein, 24 carbs, 0.8g fiber
Using Peanut flour & erythritol = 65 calories, 6g fat, 2g protein, 1.5 carbs, 1.1g fiber

Acid Blockers

So many people are popping TUMS or acid blockers like they were an "after-dinner mint." I want you to understand there are so many side effects to these. When you have acid reflex, what is happening is poor digestion, in part because the food you are eating no longer contains the enzymes needed to digest it. Foods that sit on the shelf don't need or want the enzymes that help ripen the food. To put it into perspective, corn from the garden may have a shelf life of 4 to 6 days, BUT the corn-filled tortilla chips in your pantry last forever. Most people don't need acid blockers after eating healthy veggies, it is usually after indulging in chips, cereal, and foods that are devoid of enzymes; they are very hard to digest.

Does this describe you, or someone you know…You are at a family BBQ and you fill your plate with a brat with a large fluffy bun, side of baked beans, a handful of chips, a lemonade to wash it all down, and angel food cake with sugar-free Cool Whip for dessert. You may think this sounds like a 'normal' meal, but to your stomach, all of this food is filled with foreign preservatives and chemicals. Add to this all of the conversation from family which leads to inadequate chewing and low levels of digestive enzymes will cause this gooey mix of "food" to lay in the stomach to ferment, which causes the stomach to expand and increase gas. As the gas rises, it gets trapped in the esophagus causing swelling and chest pain. This pressure overloads the stomach and pulls the gastro esophageal valve to the point where it opens. This abused valve allows stomach acid up into the esophagus. The esophagus doesn't contain acid secreting cells like the stomach so this causes burning in the esophagus, which can mimic signs of a heart attack.

The stomach has cells that secrete acid; it is required to breakdown proteins into its usable pieces of amino acids. When acid production is inhibited, food isn't digested. Instead, food remains in the stomach, fermenting by bacteria. The undigested brat bun (carbohydrates) ferments, undigested chips (fats) become rancid and the undigested brat (proteins) putrefy. This causes bloating, gas, and indigestion and over time malnutrition. When we go down the path of eating foods devoid of live nutrients, it results in acid reflux and any acid in the stomach hurts. Prescription antacids decrease the pain but not without consequences. Antacids actually become addictive, resulting in a massive increase in stomach acid when you stop them. Your body constantly tries to make stomach acid (when you take anti-acid meds because you NEED IT), so it pumps out extra levels of a hormone called Gastrin that stimulates stomach acid. Therefore, when you stop antacids, the stomach makes huge amounts of acid. Which the pharmaceutical companies love because you are now addicted and don't know what else to do. If you still think the problem is too much acid, think about this….The older people get the more likely they are to use antacids. This is interesting as stomach acid production decreases as people get older and we produce less digestive enzymes (which is why we lose the ability to taste foods).

SIDE EFFECTS OF ACID BLOCKERS

1. FOOD ALLERGIES - When you don't have stomach acid to breakdown food, undigested proteins sit like a rock in the intestines. This slowly eats holes in your intestines and this inflammation begins a detrimental snowball effect. When you start to have holes in your intestines, food starts to leak into your bloodstream (leaky gut syndrome). This is awful because the immune system goes into overdrive to kill the unknown substances in the blood. If you are a fan of cereal and milk, you will most likely have a wheat and dairy allergy.

2. OSTEOPOROSIS - Without stomach acid, your body isn't able to digest food properly and you become nutritionally deficient. You can't strip the calcium from your food and this will weaken your bones.

3. METABOLISM - They block the absorption of thyroid hormone.

4. REFLUX - Ironically, blocking stomach acid may also contribute to acid reflux!

5. IRON and B-12 DEFICIENCY - You can't absorb iron (which is essential for carrying oxygen to the mitochondria of our cells). An iron deficiency = restless legs, low energy, decreased ability to oxidize fat when you work out! BAD BAD BAD. B-12 DEFICIENCY can cause anemia, fatigue, constipation, brain fog, and nerve issues. One of my clients couldn't feel his feet because of over use of acid blockers.

6. FOOD POISONING - One of the main jobs of stomach acid is to kill harmful pathogens that may be present in the food before they can make you sick. If you consistently take acid blockers, you are susceptible to food poisoning.

STEPS TO HEAL

1. Drink small amounts of room temperature water while eating. Drinking large amounts of cold beverages dilutes your digestive enzymes.

2. Skip the coffee, carbonated beverages, alcohol and aspirin until your intestines are healed.

3. Add in Aloe Vera supplements; it naturally repairs the damage that was done to the esophagus safely. Aloe Vera's major ingredient buffers pH+ and it naturally speeds the healing process.

4. DECREASE foods that cause the problems: food chemicals, vegetable oils, sugar, and starch. It could also be a food allergy/sensitivity; in this case eliminate gluten or the food causing the issue.

5. Eat foods that heal the intestines: coconut oil, bone broth, and any "healthified" recipe that has no sugar.

6. Add in supplements to heal the intestines so you can enjoy food again! Check out the book: Secrets to a Healthy Metabolism to read more on supplements. Licorice, l-glutamine, probiotics, digestive enzymes, aloe vera and other supplements can heal your intestinal wall.

Thyroid Health

Many Americans suffer from symptoms such as cold hands and feet, low body temperature, sensitivity to cold, a feeling of always being chilled, headaches, insomnia, dry skin, puffy eyes, hair loss, brittle nails, joint aches, constipation, mental dullness, fatigue, frequent infections, hoarse voice, ringing in the ears, dizziness, loss of libido, and weight gain, which is sometimes uncontrollable. Research is pointing to the fact that an under active thyroid might be the number one cause of weight problems, especially among women, in the US today.

Many dietary oils can negatively affect thyroid health. We cook with them almost every day and they are plentiful in commercially prepared foods. It is possible they are among the worst offenders when it comes to the thyroid. They are known as vegetable oils or polyunsaturated oils. The most common source of these oils used in commercially prepared foods is the soybean.

Unsaturated oils block thyroid hormone secretion, its movement in the circulatory system, and the response of tissues to the hormone. When the thyroid hormone is deficient, the body is generally exposed to increased levels of estrogen. The thyroid hormone is essential for making the 'protective hormones' progesterone and pregnenolone, so these hormones are lowered when anything interferes with the function of the thyroid. The thyroid hormone is required for using and eliminating cholesterol, so cholesterol is likely to be raised by anything which blocks the thyroid function.

Coconut oil, on the other hand, is a saturated fat made up primarily of medium chain fatty acids. Also known as medium chain triglycerides (MCTs), medium chain fatty acids are known to increase metabolism and promote weight loss. Coconut oil can also raise basal body temperatures while increasing metabolism. This is good news for people who suffer with low thyroid function.

So here is my thyroid-supporting zucchini bread....

Sweet Zucchini Bread

Ingredients:

1 c. shredded zucchini

10 eggs

3/4 c. butter or
    coconut oil, melted

1/4 c. erythritol

1 tsp stevia glycerite

2 tsp cinnamon

1 tsp nutmeg

1/2 tsp ginger

1 tsp Celtic sea salt

1 cup coconut flour

1 tsp aluminum free
    baking powder

1 tsp vanilla extract

Directions:

Preheat oven to 350 degrees F. In a large bowl combine zucchini, eggs, sweetener, cinnamon and spices. In a separate bowl, mix together coconut flour and baking powder, then stir into the wet ingredients just until smooth. Stir in the vanilla. Grease a loaf pan (9x5x3) with coconut oil spray, pour mixture into pan and bake for 65-75 minutes.

Makes 12 slices.
NUTRITIONAL COMAPARISON (per slice)
Traditional Zucchini Bread = 424 calories, 14g fat, 3g protein, 58 carbs, 2g fiber
"Healthified" Zucchini Bread = 211 calories, 16g fat, 7g protein, 6 carbs, 4g fiber

Low Fat Diet Facts

It is more about WHAT you are putting in your body. Dipping tlow in calories is so detrimental to our metabolism. You will lose weight, but when you go back to eating your metabolism will be slower than when you started. Our muscles need amino acids. When we cut calories (and it is usually protein and fat that is first to go), our muscles become cannibals! Our bodies need amino acids continually throughout the day. If you stop eating protein, your body starts to eat your muscles! One pound of muscle burns about 50 calories per day and one pound of fat burns only 2...even when you are sleeping!

LOW CALORIE DIETS, Why you lose weight:

---

1 lb. of muscle provides only 600 calories,
while, 1 lb. of fat provides 3,500 calories.

If you go on a daily calorie deficit of 500 calories;
that comes to 3,500 calories per week (500 x 7 = 3,500).

If all of those calories came from fat, you'd lose just 1 pound.
IF the calories came from muscle, you'd lose 6 pounds.

So, 100% fat loss is the equivalent of 1 pound of weight lost,
while 100% muscle loss is the equivalent of 6 pounds.

The Low Fat diets will help you lose weight on the scale BUT, losing muscle = slower metabolism!!!
1 lb of muscle burns 50 calories/day vs 2 calories/day for fat.

SO after a fast or low calorie diet, you no longer will be able to eat like you once could;
you have to eat less and less to maintain your weight! NO THANK YOU...

There are lots of different types of amino acids. Consuming the right ones at certain times of the day can REALLY enhance fat loss! Some amino acids shuttle fat to the mitochondria where you burn fat, so taking that before a workout doubles your loss. Some amino acids aid in muscle recovery, while others increase the Human Growth Hormone while you sleep (fat burning hormone).

Cinnamon Fry Bread

Ingredients:

3 eggs, separated

Coconut oil/butter/or
  ghee for frying

1/4 c. vanilla egg white/
  whey protein

1 tsp vanilla/almond/or
  maple extract

1/4 c. cinnamon

3 TBS erythritol

1 tsp stevia glycerite

Directions...

Separate the eggs (save the yolks for a different recipe), and whip the whites in a clean, dry, cool bowl for a few minutes until VERY stiff. Blend in the whey protein and extract. Heat the oil in a frying pan on medium high until a drop of water will sizzle. Once it is hot, place a circle of dough on the pan. Fry until golden brown on both sides. Remove from heat and place on a plate. Sprinkle with cinnamon and sweetener. ENJOY!

Makes 6 servings.
NUTRITIONAL COMPARISON (per serving)
Traditional Fry Bread = 217 calories, 22g fat, 2g protein, 32 carbs, 0g fiber
"Healthified" Fry Brtead = 168 calories, 11g fat, 17g protein, 0.8 carbs, 0g fiber

Hazelnut Muffins

Ingredients:

2 c. hazelnut meal
    (or other nut)
1 c. freshly ground
    flaxseeds
2 tsp aluminum free
    baking powder
1/4 tsp Celtic sea salt
1 tsp cinnamon
1/2 c. Erythritol
1 tsp stevia glycerite
2 tsp vanilla extract
1/2 c. unsweetened
    almond milk
1/4 c. coconut oil
    or butter, melted
4 eggs

STREUSEL:

1 c. hazelnut meal (or other nut)
1/4 c. erythritol and ½ tsp stevia glycerite
1 TBS cinnamon
1/8 tsp Celtic sea salt
1/4 c. chilled butter or cocount oil

Directions...

Preheat oven to 350. Grease muffin pan. In a medium sized bowl, mix streusel ingredients until crumbly. Set aside. In another bowl, mix all muffin batter ingredients together. Put a thin layer of muffin batter into each muffin cup. Add a tablespoon of streusel, top with another layer of muffin batter, then top this with the remaining streusel. Bake for 18-20 minutes or until set.

Makes 12 servings.

NUTRITIONAL COMPARISON (per serving):
Traditional Hazelnut Muffin = 290 calories, 15g fat, 1g protein, 29 carbs, 0g fiber
"Healthified" Hazelnut Muffin = 280 calories, 26g fat, 7g protein, 7.5 carbs, 5.8g fiber (1.3 effective carbs)

Ingredients:

1/2 c. coconut oil
　or butter
1/2 c. erythritol
1 tsp stevia glycerite
3 eggs, beaten
1/2 c. natural
　peanut butter
3/4 c. sour cream
1 tsp vanilla extract
2 c. peanut flour
1 tsp baking powder
1 tsp baking soda
1/2 tsp Celtic sea salt
1 ChocoPerfection Bar,
　chopped

Directions:

Preheat oven to 350 degrees F. Cream butter and sweetener. Beat eggs in well. Mix in peanut butter, sour cream, and vanilla. Combine peanut flour, baking powder, soda and salt together and add to creamed mixture. Stir in most of the chocolate chips, reserving a few for the top. Spoon mixture into greased mini muffin tin. Place in oven for 10-12 minutes. Test with a toothpick for doneness.

(Dairy allergy: see pg. 9)

Makes 12 large muffins or 42 mini muffins.
NUTRITIONAL COMPARISON (per 1 large cupcake)

Traditional Muffins = 396 calories, 20g fat, 6g protein, 49.5 carbs, 2.5g fiber

"Healthified" Muffin (makes 12 servings) =
302 calories, 18g fat, 10g protein, 12 carbs, 6.9g fiber

"Healthified" Minis (makes 42 muffins) =
86 calories, 5g fat, 2.8g protein, 3.6 carbs, 2g fiber

Migraine and Serotonin

A migraine is your body's way of telling you that something is wrong, this isn't the way our brains are meant to work. Approximately 1 out of every 10 Americans experience migraines, with women being affected 3 times more often than men. A variety of factors can trigger migraines. Triggers include over-use of headache medications, magnesium deficiency, FOOD ALLERGIES and sensitivities, tyramine containing foods, low serotonin, blood sugar imbalances, low thyroid, inflammation from tran-fats and too many carbohydrates, food dyes and chemicals, sleep issues, LOTS of things that can be controlled by our diet! Research has linked the migraine headaches with imbalances in our neurotransmitters, specifically serotonin. This is why women suffer more often than men, our serotonin drops during our menstrual cycle...have you noticed the migraines come during certain 'times of the month?' Serotonin plays many roles in the body, and it has an effect on blood vessels. When serotonin levels are high, blood vessels constrict (shrink).

When serotonin levels fall, the blood vessels dilate (swell). This swelling can cause pain or other problems. Many things can affect the level of serotonin in your body, including your level of blood sugar, certain foods and changes in your estrogen level. Tryptophan is a precursor to serotonin and is a naturally-occurring substance that can be found in a variety of foods. Tryptophan must enter the brain by crossing the blood-brain barrier. This barrier, made of brain capillary walls, prevents the passage of bacteria, viruses and some drugs, yet permitting glucose and amino acids to pass through. Foods high in tryptophan that can cross the blood-brain barrier are sesame seeds, sunflower seeds, eggs, edamame, cheddar cheese, pork chops, caribou, turkey, and whey protein. The commercially available alpha-lactalbumin, a whey protein and the primary protein in human breast milk, is high in tryptophan. To produce more serotonin, aim to get at least two daily servings of animal protein like poultry, eggs and shrimp per day. Each serving of these foods provides the body with about 300 mg of tryptophan, the amino acid needed to produce serotonin. For best results, take 5-HTP supplement to increase serotonin before bed. It converts tryptophan into serotonin during the sleep cycle. Researchers at the University of Cambridge in the United Kingdom found that a daily dose of 500 mg boosted levels of serotonin within two weeks. Please note: if you are taking a prescription anti-depressant, you shouldn't take 5-HTP. Other supplements such as high doses of magnesium are also a necessity to calm migraines. Let's try this recipe filled with eggs for serotonin and blood sugar balancing coconut flour!

Ingredients:

1/2 c. coconut flour

1/4 c. psyllium husk

1/4 tsp Celtic sea salt

1/4 tsp baking soda

6 eggs

1/2 c. erythritol

1 tsp stevia glycerite

1 tsp vanilla or lemon oil

1/2 c. coconut oil
or butter, melted

1/4 c. poppy seeds

1/3 c. lemon juice

1 TBS grated lemon zest

LEMON GLAZE:

1/2 tsp stevia glycerite (or more to taste)

1/2 c. cream cheese or coconut cream

1/2 c. lemon juice

1 tsp vanilla extract and a pinch Celtic sea salt

Directions . . . Preheat oven to 350 degrees F. In a medium sized bowl sift together the dry ingredients. Slowly add the wet ingredients into the dry ingredients and stir until very smooth. Grease a muffin pan and fill about 2/3 of the way full with batter. Bake for 18-20 minutes, or until a toothpick comes out clean. For the glaze, blend all ingredients until smooth. Drizzle on top of muffins.

Makes 12 muffins.

NUTRITIONAL COMPARISON (per muffin)

Krusteaz Muffins = 225 calories, 14g fat, 2g protein, 36.2 carbs, 0.9g fiber

"Healthified" Muffin = 199 calories, 16g fat, 5g protein, 4.9 carbs, 3.1g fiber

Tired Toxic Liver

Your liver plays a major role in weight loss. The liver is a chief organ in the body for metabolism functions. Keeping our liver at optimal health should be a main focus of your weight loss plan. I write a chapter in my book, Secrets to a Healthy Metabolism, called Tired Toxic Liver...this is my mom's favorite sub-chapter because it all makes sense!

The liver makes and secretes bile for storage in the gallbladder. During digestion, the bile is moved to the intestine to break down fats. But, if the liver is congested, it doesn't produce enough bile for fat to be broken down. The liver can become congested from chemicals, toxins, drugs and heavy metals. Evidence of a "fatty liver" is often shown by a roll of fat at the waistline, which happens because the liver has stopped breaking down fat and started storing it. Only once you bring your liver back to full function, will you lose this fat. This is why I list specific ingredients like "aluminum free baking powder." All of these steps help the body in little, yet important ways.

When the liver is overloaded and toxic, every organ in a person's body is affected and weight loss efforts are stalled. Some signs of a toxic liver are weight gain, cellulite, abdominal bloating, indigestion, fatigue, mood swings, depression, high blood pressure, elevated cholesterol, and skin rashes. Many people struggle with weight gain and a sluggish metabolism most of their lives, and go through lots of yo-yo dieting unsuccessfully. "So why doesn't anything really work?" we may ask. We have been tackling the symptom when we should be addressing the cause; weight gain is often due to poor liver function.

The liver performs more than 400 different jobs, and is the body's most important metabolism-enhancing organ; it acts as a filter to clear the body of toxins, metabolize protein, control hormonal balance and enhance our immune system. Your liver is a "worker bee" that can even regenerate its own damaged cells! But our liver is not invincible. When it is abused and lacks essential nutrients, or when it is overwhelmed by toxins, it no longer performs as it should. Fat may build up in the liver and just under the skin, hormone imbalances can develop, and toxins increase and get into the blood stream.

The liver metabolizes not only fats, but proteins and carbohydrates for fuel. It breaks down amino acids from proteins into various pieces to help build muscle; which directly impacts your calorie burn. It also transports amino acids through the blood stream for hormone balance; which is critical to avoid water retention, bloating, cravings, as well other undesired weight issues. Amino acids also help move waste, such as damaged cholesterol, and used estrogen and insulin to the liver, for detoxification and elimination through the kidney.

The liver's most important function, and the one that puts it at greatest risk for damages, is to detoxify the numerous toxins that attack our bodies daily. Working together with the lungs, kidneys, skin and

intestines, a healthy liver detoxifies many damaging substances and eliminates them without polluting the bloodstream. When we cleanse the liver and eat the right foods, liver metabolism will improve and we start burning fat. As liver function improves, so does energy. With more energy, fitness improves, because we have the ability to exercise more and improve our muscle tone.

The following are the most common symptoms of a toxic liver; being edgy, easily stressed, elevated cholesterol, skin irritation, depression, sleep difficulties, indigestion, kidney damage, heart damage, brain fog, hypothyroidism, chronic fatigue, weight gain, poor memory, PMS, blood sugar imbalances, allergies, or obesity. The liver also plays a role in migraines. If this vital organ is overloaded with toxic substances, it can cause inflammation that triggers migraine pain. If you have tried many ways to improve your health and energy level and nothing seemed to help, it is possible that your tired liver is triggering your difficulties. Restoring liver function is one of the most essential actions you could ever do for your health. When the liver gets congested it will remain that way and get worse until it gets cleaned and revitalized.

THINGS TO AVOID

1. FRUCTOSE: Grabbing a banana for breakfast is a bad thing to do for your liver, yet so many people do this thinking it is helpful for weight loss. Fructose, the sugar in fruit is really hard on our liver. Think of fruit (and only the low-sugar berries) as an occasional treat. Agave is 90% fructose.
2. SUGAR: You may say you don't consume sugar, but you may be ingesting it from a lot of prepared food unknowingly. It is hidden in marinara sauce, ketchup, salad dressings, the list is scary. In the process of being metabolized, sugar robs your body of important nutrients; for example zinc, is essential for liver function. Sugar also restrains your liver's production of enzymes.
3. HYDROGENATED OILS: Trans-fat obstructs your liver's ability to burn fat. Our body will never learn how to process those "plastic-like", man-made fats.
4. Some liver stressors are caffeine, sugars, trans-fats, chocolate, soft drinks, many over the counter medications, cholesterol lowering drugs, anticonvulsants, and an inadequate intake of fiber. Women detoxify caffeine slower than men because of hormonal interactions with caffeine. Birth control pills also increase the time to detox caffeine by twice as much.
5. ALCOHOL: Alcohol interferes with the liver's ability to metabolize hormones, which are important for maintaining blood pressure. Having one drink can cause acute liver inflammation. As the liver breaks down alcohol, by-products are formed, such as acetaldehyde. Drinking alcohol depletes a store of a liver peptide called GHS, which helps us detoxify chemicals. The cell damage that occurs is caused by free radicals, highly reactive molecular fragments, liberated during alcohol metabolism.

Protein and Metabolism

The most important piece of our thermic effect of food metabolism is the amount of quality protein in our diets; which influences weight loss. Protein helps us sustain muscle during weight loss, improve muscle strength and endurance, improve immunity, enhance antioxidant function, build HDL cholesterol, and helps insulin and leptin functions; all of which will help maximize our metabolism.

A higher-protein diet also has a natural diuretic effect. People with extra weight are often sluggish and holding extra water; which can cause blood pressure go up and causes our heart to push harder to move the stagnation. The extra water in connective tissues directly gets in the way of fat burning. When you eat a higher protein diet, an important blood protein called albumin increases; which, draws water back out of your connective tissues and helps you get rid of fluid retention. If you have too much inflammation, your kidneys may leak albumin into your urine, provoking fluid retention, weight problems, and considerable cardiovascular risk. When we eat too many carbohydrates and not enough protein, the opposite happens; we retain more fluids. It also stimulates too much leptin; provoking leptin resistance and an intense desire for more carbohydrates. Too many carbohydrates cause your willpower to be in a constant battle with out-of-balance leptin. It is pretty obvious from the amount of yo-yo dieting in our culture that misguided leptin usually wins. The best way to win the battle is to not have it in the first place, meaning don't eat too many carbohydrates and more importantly, not by themselves.

I see a lot of clients come to me after trying a well-known popular diet, (which I won't name, but they count points) which worked for a while, but they are stuck at a weight they are still uncomfortable at. Counting points isn't helpful for our biochemistry…they concentrate on calories. Saving up all your points for a Blizzard isn't going to enhance your physique; even if you only eat 800 calories a day…it is 800 calories of trans-fat filled sugar! Culver's has a Pumpkin Cheesecake Concrete Mixer with a medium size carrying just a smidge under 1,000 calories and over 100g of carbs! Yikes, I will make mine at home!

Ingredients:

1 cup vanilla almond milk

1/2 c. canned pumpkin

2 oz cream cheese
   or coconut cream

2 TBS Just Like Sugar or
   1 tsp stevia glycerite

1 scoop vanilla whey/
   egg white protein

1 c. crushed ice

Directions: Place all ingredients in a blender, blend until very smooth, sweeten to taste and enjoy!

NUTRITIONAL COMPARISON (per serving)

Culver's Pumpkin Mixer = 993 calories, 53g fat, 16g protein, 113g carbs, 2g fiber,

"Healthified" Mixer = 365 calories, 18g fat, 29g protein, 8.5 carbs, 2g fiber

OPTIONAL FOR ADDED FLAVOR:

1/4 tsp each of nutmeg, ginger, cinnamon and ground cloves

OR 1 tsp pumpkin pie spice

Alzheimer's and Choline

Do you know anyone suffering from Alzheimer's? How is your memory? Do you only eat egg whites? If you are, you are skimping on an essential mineral called CHOLINE! Egg yolks are filled with this vital mineral. Choline is a chemical similar to the B-vitamins and serves many functions in our bodies:

1. Composes the structure of cell membranes, the flexibility and integrity depend on adequate supplies of choline.

2. Protects our livers from accumulating fat. 77% of men, 80% of postmenopausal women, and 44% of premenopausal women developed fatty liver when they ate a diet deprived of choline. (Premenopausal women are not as affected because choline can be made by our bodies from the synthesis of phosphatidyl-choline, which is regulated by estrogen from our ovaries).

3. It is the precursor molecule for the neurotransmitter acetylcholine. This is a neurotransmitter that carries messages from and to nerves, acetylcholine is the body's primary chemical means of sending messages between nerves and muscles.

4. Because of rapid development in fetuses and infants, we have a great need for choline in our early lives. Human milk has high levels of choline. Studies prove that mothers who don't consume enough choline have babies with less brain development and poorer memories after birth.

I know, I know, you are asking, "Well, how many eggs can I have in a day? What about the cholesterol in the yolks?" When most people hear "cholesterol" they think "bad." Like most things in life, the reality is more complex. First off, I am talking about using farm-fresh, free-range, omega-3 filled eggs. Yes, they cost more, but I don't need to buy Choline or Omega 3 supplements...I just spend my money on quality food!

Cholesterol is more of our "fire-fighters" that come in to put out the inflammation going on in our body. If your cholesterol numbers are high, you have inflammation going on. So instead of forcefully pushing cholesterol down with statin drugs, focus on what is causing the inflammation. People whose diets supplied the highest average intake of choline (egg yolks), have levels of inflammatory markers at least 20% lower than people with the lowest intakes, reports the American Journal of Clinical Nutrition (Detopoulou P, Panagiotakos DB, et al.) Chronic inflammation has been linked to a wide range of conditions including cognitive decline and Alzheimer's, heart disease, osteoporosis, and type-2 diabetes. Inflamation is caused by an omega 3 imbalance, oxidized milk solids added to skim/1%/2% milk, trans-fat, food allergies, alcohol consumption, and fructose (Agave, HFCS, JUICE).

mE
Maria Emmerich

Chocolate Cream Puffs

Ingredients:

3 eggs, separated
1/8 tsp cream of tartar
1/2 c. chocolate whey/
   egg protein
4 TBS cocoa powder
3 oz cream cheese
½ tsp stevia glycerite

FILLING:
2 c. raw hazelnuts
1/2 c. unsweetened
   cocoa powder
1/2 c. erythritol
1 tsp stevia
1/2 tsp vanilla
1/8 tsp Celtic sea salt
3 TBS hazelnut oil
   (or macadamia oil)

Directions... Preheat oven to 300 degrees F. In a bowl,

whip egg whites with cream of tartar until peaks are very stiff. Slowly mix in whey protein and cocoa powder. In separate bowl, blend cream cheese, yolks and stevia. Slowly add the cream cheese mixture into the stiff egg whites. Grease a cookie sheet or a medium size muffin tin. Bake for 20 minutes (or until golden brown). Remove pans from oven and let cool on a cooling rack. Once cool, use a knife to cut a small hole in the puffs to insert the cream filling. (Dairy allergy: see pg. 9)

FILLING: In a food processor, grind the hazelnuts to a smooth butter, scraping the sides as needed so they process evenly, about 5 minutes. Add all the filling ingredients and continue to process until well blended. If it is too dry, add in a little extra hazelnut oil until the desired consistency is achieved. Remove to a container, cover and refrigerate until needed. Bring to room temperature before using.

NUTRITIONAL COMPARISON:
Traditional Nutella Puffs = 212 calories, 15g fat, 5g protein, 23 carbs, 3g fiber
"Healthified" Puffs = 126 calories, 12g fat, 5g protein, 2 carbs, 1g fiber

Oils

One reason why trans-fats are so bad is that they interfere with our cell's ability to metabolize OMEGA 3 fats. Our brain = 60% fat. Trans-fats damage cell membranes of vital structures of our brain and nerve cells.

Imagine this: We have "parking spots" that are specifically designed to receive certain molecules. When OMEGA 3's "park", it fills assigned parking spot and contributes to the health of the membrane. However, if trans fatty acid "cars" come along, they try to squeeze into a space that doesn't fit. A biochemical traffic jam occurs and the right cars can't get to where they need to be.

2 PROBLEMS OCCUR:

1. The molecular misfit "car" is left to wander throughout the body, causing damage in other places.
2. These misfit "cars" keep pushing their way in, damaging them and the "cars" around them. This also changes the cellular membrane and the right "cars", the healthy nutrients, no longer fit.

Hydrogenated fats can weaken cell membranes, keeping out needed nutrients and also allowing harmful ones to leak in. Causing inflammation (which will increase cholesterol)...cholesterol isn't the bad guy. Think of cholesterol as the firefighters that are trying to put out the fire (inflammation). We need to heal inflammation, NOT take a prescription drug that kills the firefighters. That is isn't going to help ....put out the fire!

Maria Emmerich

Ingredients:

"PUFFS":

3 eggs, separated

1 tsp cream of tartar

1/2 c. vanilla egg white/
    whey protein

1/2 c. pumpkin

1 tsp pumpkin spice

Stevia glycerite (to taste)

FILLING:

1/2 c. butter or
    coconut oil

8 oz cream cheese
    or coconut cream

3 TBS unsweetened
    almond milk

1 TBS Stevia Glycerite
    (OR ¼ cup erythritol)

Directions...

Preheat oven to 375 degrees. Separate the eggs and reserve the yolks for another recipe. In a large bowl, whip egg whites and cream of tartar until VERY stiff. Then add the whey. Using a spatula, gradually fold the pumpkin and spices into the egg white mixture, being careful not to break down the whites. If you want a sweeter puff, add in 1 tsp stevia. Place round balls of dough onto a GREASED baking sheet (or a mini muffin tin works great). Bake at 375 degrees for 10 minutes. Keep oven shut, and leave the puffs in there for another 5 minutes or until cool.

FILLING: If using butter, brown the butter in a sauce pan (stir constantly on high heat until light golden brown – it makes such a difference!!! Once brown add the rest of the filling ingredients. Stir until creamy. Allow to cool. Place into a large Ziplock bag or pastry filler and allow to cool further for at least 2 hours, it will thicken. Cut a small hole in the corner of the bag and use to pipe into puffs.

Makes 24 puffs.
NUTRITIONAL COMPARISON (per 2 puffs)
Traditional Pumpkin Puff = 235 calories, 18g fat, 2g protein, 12.8 carbs, 0.7g fiber
"Healthified" Puff = 160 calories, 14g fat, 5g protein, 1.4 carbs, trace fiber

Coconut and Fertility

The amazing properties of coconuts have been celebrated for their fertility and pregnancy boosting abilities. In tropical areas where coconuts are plentiful, pregnant women drink coconut water to increase the fetus' health; babies in Thailand eat 3 spoonfuls of coconut puree as their first baby food from the priest; and women in India get a special coconut from the priest for a blessing when trying to conceive. Not only were the women correct with the traditions of enhancing the babies health, but we now have scientific proof of the numerous health benefits of coconuts.

HEALTH BENEFITS OF COCONUTS

1. DECREASES MISCARRIAGES: Fat is essential to make hormones. Some miscarriages are caused by a lack of progesterone to sustain the pregnancy. Eating coconut oil in addition to progesterone supplementation will provide a healthy fat that can be used to attain a healthy body weight and balance hormones.

2. CONCEPTION: Fat is essential to make hormones. Some miscarriages are caused by a lack of progesterone to sustain the pregnancy. Overweight women may have problems conceiving due to too much estrogen (we have 3 types of estrogen: I'm talking about the one stored in our fat cells); this will inhibit ovulation from happening, and decrease the lining of the uterus for implantation, along with many other imbalances. Coconut oil is a medium-chained triglyceride, which aids in thyroid health and helps women lose weight while also balancing hormones.

3. MORNING SICKNESS: Coconut water is a natural remedy for nausea and has been traditionally used to calm malaria, typhoid, and other illness that include nausea as a side effect.

4. DECREASES GAS: It naturally calms and heals the stomach lining, and eventually decreases gas.

5. HYDRATION: Coconut water is nature's true "sports drink." It has all the electrolytes and minerals that we need and lose during extreme activity (such as marathon running) and also supports the nutritional needs of pregnant women with the extra blood volume.

6. NUMBER 2: Most pregnant women struggle with going #2 in the third trimester. This is due to the intestines slowing down to absorb extra nutrients for the fetus. Coconut is a mild laxative. Coconut milk, water or eating coconut oil can assist to keep our intestinal system moving properly.

7. GESTATIONAL DIABETES: Coconut assists with proper blood sugar balance. When our blood sugar goes too high (if you eat too many crackers or processed carbs with morning sickness), your blood sugar drops too low and this will not only lead to insulin issues, it also induces nausea! Coconut will help due to the high amounts of fiber and the healthy fats keep our insulin levels from rising too much.

8. URINARY TRACK INFECTIONS: No need for antibiotics that decrease the mother's and baby's probiotics (and cause food allergies). Coconut decreases UTI's because it cleans the kidneys.

9. IMMUNE SYSTEM: Coconut oil is 50% lauric acid (LA). LA has natural antiviral, antibacterial, and antifungal properties. Pregnant women have a weakened immune system and LA boosts immunity and protects her from harmful infections.

10. BODY TEMPERATURE: Coconut cools the body, which can be an issue with the high levels of progesterone and weight.

11. STRETCH MARKS: Coconut oil is AMAZING for the skin! It moisturizes itchy and dry skin. It also reduces the appearance of stretch marks. When applied to the perineum in the weeks leading up to labor, it can help reduce tearing during birth.

12. ACNE: When applied to the skin and face, coconut water clears up acne and blackheads caused by the high levels of hormones during pregnancy.

13. LACTATION: Lauric Acid (LA) is found in two sources: coconut and breast milk! It has been proven that breast feeding women who eat coconut products have higher levels of LA in their milk. This is important because as listed above, it boosts the immune system. Other awesome properties of LA is that it increases the baby's brain and bone development. Our bodies can store LA so start consuming coconut early on in pregnancy to help with milk production.

PEANUT BUTTER DONUT: Recipe on page 41.

Cholesterol Facts

Did you know that cholesterol levels are a very poor predictor of future heart attacks? The risk of future heart attacks has everything to do with excess levels of insulin. This is why diabetics are known to be at a high risk of heart disease. Scientists used to think we had to worry only about our total cholesterol level, but then researchers found this wasn't a very strong predictor of heart disease. Next came the realization that there was both "good" (HDL) and "bad" (LDL) cholesterol. This launched a war against "bad" cholesterol, which is predominantly elevated by saturated fat. We now know that there are 2 types of LDL cholesterol:

1. Large, fluffy LDL particles that appear to have no potential to cause atherosclerosis or the development of plaques on the large or medium-sized arteries.

2. Small, dense LDL particles that are strongly associated with arterial plaques and this can increase the risk of heart disease.

To determine which type of LDL = find your ratio of triglycerides to HDL cholesterol.

-If ratio is less than 2, you have fluffy LDL particles that are not going to do you much harm.

-If ratio is greater than 4, you have small-dense LDL particles that increase the development of atherosclerotic plaques – regardless of your total cholesterol levels.

Harvard Medical School has confirmed the importance of this ratio; the higher your TG/HDL ratio, the more likely you would be to have a heart attack. In some cases 16 times more likely! Improve your TG/HDL ratio in 2 ways.

1. Lower your insulin levels. Excess insulin = increase triglyceride levels. Eat the "healthified" way!

2. Supplement with high-dose, ultra refined-grade fish oils at every meal.

Cholesterol statins are also powerful anti-inflammatory agents, but not without consequences. They do lower C-reactive proteins; they worked like aspirin to reduce inflammation and therefore reduce heart attacks. Only statins cost a lot more and are less effective. The statins also include some serious side effects:

1. Muscle wasting = slower metabolism = higher triglycerides = snowball effect

2. Decrease cholesterol-production in brain = decreased production of new synaptic connections and loss of memory.

Combining a low carb diet to control insulin with high-dose fish oil (to decrease inflammation) is the answer to decreasing risk of heart disease.

Ingredients:

5 oz cream cheese or
  coconut cream, softened

3/4 c. coconut oil or
  butter, softened

1 TBS vanilla extract

4 large eggs

1/2 c. coconut flour

1 c. erythritol

1 tsp stevia glycerite

1/2 tsp Celtic sea salt

1/4 tsp aluminum free
  baking powder

2/3 c. unsweetened
  almond milk

1/2 c. chopped pecans

Directions...

Preheat oven to 350 degrees. Brush both sides of an 8" by 8" pan with coconut oil, or spray with coconut oil cooking spray. In a large bowl, beat softened cream cheese with electric mixer until smooth. Mix in butter, vanilla, and sweetener. Whisk together dry ingredients. Add eggs one at a time to cream cheese mixture, and beat until smooth. Add dry ingredients and almond milk. Fold in nuts. Pour mixture into prepared pan, and smooth top with a spatula. Bake at 350 degrees for 45 minutes until toothpick inserted in center comes out clean.

Makes 16 servings.
NUTRITIONAL COMPARISON (per serving)
Traditional Blondie = 325 calories, 17g fat, 2g protein, 35 carbs, 1.2g fiber
"Healthified" Blondie = 164 calories, 17g fat, 4g protein, 3 carbs, 1.8g fiber

BROWNIE VARIATION: add 1/3 cup unsweetened cocoa powder to the dry mix and 2 ounces finely chopped unsweetened baking chocolate to the cream cheese mixture.

Maria Emmerich

Chocolate Chip Cookie

Ingredients:

1/2 c. butter or coconut oil

1 egg

1/2 c. Just Like Sugar

1/4 c. erythritol

1 tsp stevia glycerite

3/4 c. blanched almond flour

1/4 c. coconut flour

1/2 tsp aluminum free
      baking powder

1 tsp Celtic sea salt

1 ChocoPerfection Bar
  (chopped)

Directions: Preheat the oven to 325 degrees F.

In a medium bowl, cream the butter, egg, Just Like Brown Sugar, erythritol and stevia. Cream for a few minutes until very fluffy. In a separate bowl mix together the almond flour, coconut flour, baking powder, and salt. Slowly add in the dry ingredients to the wet and mix until smooth. Add in chocolate. Roll 2 TBS of dough into a ball in your hands (for uniform shape) onto a cookie sheet, then press down until they are about ¾ of an inch thick. Place cookies about 2 inches apart. Bake in preheated oven for 17-20 minutes or until golden around the edges. Cool completely on the baking sheet before removing and enjoy!

Makes 12 cookies.

NUTRITIONAL COMPARISON (per cookie)

Traditional Cookie = 180 calories, 10g fat, 1g protein, 25 carbs, trace fiber

"Healthified" Cookie = 128 calories, 12g fat, 3g protein, 3.9 carbs, 2.4g fiber
(1.5 effective carbs)

VARIATIONS: Smoosh "healthified" ice cream in between 2 cookies for an ice cream sandwich! See page 83 for the ice cream recipe.

Boston Cream Minis

Ingredients:

1 1/2 c.blanched
   almond flour

1 tsp baking powder

1/2 tsp Celtic sea salt

6 TBS coconut oil or butter,
   softened

3/4 c. erythritol

1 tsp stevia glycerite

4 eggs

1 tsp vanilla extract

FILLING:

3 pkg. (8 oz.) cream cheese
   or coconut cream, softened

1/4 c. erythritol

1 tsp stevia glycerite

1 tsp vanilla

CHOCOLATE ICING:
See page 25.

Directions:

Preheat oven to 325°F. Grease a cupcake pan OR use cupcake liners. Sift together almond flour, baking powder, and salt into a large bowl. In another bowl, beat together butter and sweetener with an electric mixer at medium-high speed until pale and fluffy, 3 to 5 minutes. Beat in eggs 1 at a time, beating well after each addition, then beat in vanilla. Reduce speed to low, then add flour mixture until batter is just smooth. Spoon batter into pan.

CREAM FILLING: Beat cream cheese, sweetener and 1 tsp of the vanilla with electric mixer on medium speed until well blended. Place 1 rounded TBS of cream filling into the almond flour batter of each cupcake. Bake at 325°F for 18 to 24 minutes or until center is almost set. Let cool before frosting. NOTE: If using coconut cream, fill cupcakes after baking.

CHOCOLATE ICING: Place the butter and chopped chocolate in a double boiler (or in a heat safe dish over a pot of boiling water). Stir well until just melted (don't burn the chocolate!), let cool a little before adding in the cream and sweetener. Stir until smooth and thick. Use to drizzle over cooled cupcakes. YUM!

Makes 18 cupcakes.
NUTRITIONAL COMPARISON (per cupcake)
Traditional Cupcake = 231 calories, 15g fat, 2 g protein, 32.2 carbs, trace fiber
"Healthified" Cupcake = 183 calories, 20g fat. 4.5 g protein, 3 carbs, 1g fiber
(2 effective carbs)

Picky Eaters and Probiotics

Do you have a picky eater in your home that only likes bland foods like butter noodles? They are most likely low in healthy gut bacteria. You have trillions of bacteria in your digestive tract. They are a major part of your immune system. A healthy lower intestine should have about 85% of "good bacteria" to prevent the colonization of disease causing organisms like salmonella or E. coli.

When I ask someone if they take probiotics, I almost always get the response, "I eat yogurt." Yogurt only contains acidophilus, but that is only one of hundreds of friendly bacteria we need. Our bodies should have somewhere between 400 and 500 types of bacteria. And the type of yogurt is usually Yoplait Low Fat which has more sugar than a Kit Kat bar... that kind is not going to help here :)

Probiotics stop the growth of harmful bacteria which cause digestive problems (are you going #2??? You should every day!); they also improve digestion and absorption of vitamins; and enhance the immune system. The first 2 years of life are crucial for our long-term immune responses. Bacterial colonization patterns set up in the first years and continue to grow throughout our lifetime. The medications and foods that we give our kids totally affect this delicate balance. Probiotic supplementation promotes health in infants. They prevent eczema, diarrhea, diaper rash, and cradle-cap. They also decrease anemia and asthma. Probiotics lower the chances of food allergies and eliminate thrush.

In older children, probiotics have been found to reduce the severity and frequency of respiratory infections and prevent irritable bowel syndrome, diarrhea, and constipation. Kids with allergies, ADHD, Autism (entire Autism spectrum), Celiac Disease, Constipation, Diarrhea, Diabetes, Halitosis (bad breath), Eczema, Leaky Gut Syndrome can all benefit from healthy doses of probiotics. Acne would also be an indication of low good bacteria. Having a bout of diarrhea, taking an antibiotic, eating a diet high in refined carbohydrates and low in fiber as well as stress can all deplete a healthy intestinal flora. If a child has been on an antibiotic, it is extremely important to replenish the beneficial bacteria lost by taking a quality probiotics supplement.

Fermented foods contain healthful bacteria: Kombucha Tea, sour cream, buttermilk, sauerkraut, pickles, and many PLAIN yogurts (not yoplait:). But generally pasteurization has eliminated the flora found in modern food. As a result, companies are fortifying foods with probiotics in an effort to re-introduce this bacteria.

Cookie Dough Dip

Ingredients:

1/2 c. butter or coconut oil

1/3 c. Just Like Brown Sugar

1/2 c. Just Like Sugar
(or erythritol)

1 tsp stevia glycerite

1 tsp vanilla extract

8 oz cream cheese
or coconut cream, softened

2 ChocoPerfection Bars,
chopped

Directions

In a small saucepan, melt butter over medium heat. Add Just Like Brown Sugar and sweeteners until sweeteners dissolve and the mixture bubbles just a little. Using a hand mixer on low speed, add in vanilla and cream cheese. Mix until combined. Once the mixture is totally cool (you don't want the chocolate to melt), stir in the chuncks of ChocoPerfection. Serve with Jicama Chips. (Dairy allergy: see pg. 9)

Jicama Chips: Peel the jicama. Slice into 1/8 inch slices, then quarter the jicama into chip shapes. Enjoy!

Makes 12 servings.

NUTRITIONAL COMPARISON (per serving)

Using regular sugars = 281 calories, 20g fat, 3g protein, 22 carbs, 0.7g fiber

Using "healthy" sugar = 159 calories, 20g fat, 3g protein, 5 carbs, 4.5g fiber
(0.5 effective carbs)

Magnesium Facts

What mineral is needed by every cell in the body, yet odds are you don't get enough of it? Hint: It's not calcium. Give up? It's magnesium. It gets little attention now, but rising evidence implies that magnesium benefits your heart and bones, plus it helps prevent diabetes and migraine headaches.

Magnesium deficiencies correlate to Alzheimer's and Parkinson's. Deficiencies also cause muscle spasms, pain, insomnia and fatigue. Magnesium assists in maintaining muscle mass, nerve function, a regular heart beat, helps our immune system, and keeps bones strong. Diabetics benefit from magnesium as it helps regulate blood sugar levels. In addition, it normalizes blood pressure, and is known to be involved in energy metabolism and protein synthesis. There has been a lot of medical interest in using magnesium to avoid and manage disorders such as cardiovascular disease, diabetes, and hypertension. Diabetes is the result of insufficient production or use of insulin. Insulin converts sugar and starches in our diet into energy. Magnesium plays a significant function in carbohydrate metabolism by assisting the release and activity of insulin. A magnesium deficiency aggravates insulin resistance, a condition that starts the ball rolling for diabetes, and deficiencies are commonly found in patients with type 2 diabetes. Kidneys possibly lose their ability to maintain magnesium levels during periods of elevated levels of blood glucose. Magnesium is lost during the increased urination. Supplementing with a therapeutic dose of magnesium may improve insulin levels.

The health of our digestive system and the kidneys is jeopardized if we are deficient in magnesium. Magnesium influences metabolism, diabetes, and high blood pressure; all of which increases the probability that magnesium influences cardiovascular disease. Higher magnesium levels help reduce the risk of having a stroke. Evidence also proves that low levels of magnesium increase the risk of abnormal heart rhythms, which adds to the risk of complications after a heart attack.

Early signs of magnesium deficiency include nausea, fatigue, or weakness. As magnesium deficiency gets worse, restless leg syndrome, numbness, muscle cramps, seizures, mood changes, or irregular heartbeats can occur. Severe magnesium deficiency can also deplete the levels of calcium in the blood. Americans have the highest dietary intake of calcium in the world, yet we have the highest rate of hip fractures…hmmm, could a magnesium deficiency be the cause? Magnesium deficiency is also associated with low levels of potassium in the blood. We should get at least 400mg of magnesium a day. Are you getting enough? Highest food source is halibut with about 90mg per 3 ounces. The second highest is almonds at 80mg per ounce.

Ingredients:

MACAROONS:

2 c. blanched almonds

1/2 c. erythritol

1 tsp stevia glycerite

3 large egg whites

3/4 tsp Celtic sea salt

3 TBS erythritol

GANACHE:

3 oz unsweetened
    chocolate, chopped

1/3 c. unsweetened
    almond milk

1 TBS coconut oil
    or butter, softened

1/3 c. erythritol

1 tsp stevia glycerite

1/16 tsp raspberry extract

Directions:

Line 2 baking sheets with parchment paper. Pulse almonds with 1/2 cup Sweetener in a food processor until very finely ground, 2 to 3 minutes, then transfer to a bowl (or use blanched almond flour). In another bowl, beat egg whites with an electric mixer at medium speed until they just hold soft peaks. Add 3 TBS Sweetener and salt, a little at a time, beating, then increase speed to high and continue to beat until whites just hold stiff, glossy peaks. Stir almond mixture into meringue with a rubber spatula until completely incorporated. (Meringue will deflate.) Spoon batter into bag, pressing out excess air, and snip off 1 corner of plastic bag to create a 1/4-inch opening. Twist bag firmly just above batter, then pipe peaked mounds of batter (the size of a chocolate kiss) onto lined sheets about 1 1/2 inches apart. Let cookies stand, uncovered, at room temperature until tops are no longer sticky and a light crust forms, 20 to 30 minutes. Preheat oven to 300°F. Bake cookies for 20-30 minutes or until crisp and edges are just slightly darker. Cool completely on sheets on racks, about 30 minutes.

GANACHE: Melt chocolate with milk in a metal bowl set over a pan of barely simmering water or in top of a double boiler, stirring until smooth. (Bowl should not touch water.) Remove bowl from heat, then add oil/ butter, sweetener and raspberry extract, stirring until butter is melted. Let stand at room temperature until cooled completely and slightly thickened. Carefully peel cookies from parchment (they will be fragile). Sandwich a thin layer of ganache (about 1/2 teaspoon) between flat sides of cookies.

Makes 24 sandwich cookies. NUTRITIONAL COMPARISON (per serving)
Traditional Macaroons = 105 calories, 6.5g fat, 2.6g protein, 12 carbs, 1.6g fiber
"Healthified" Macaroons = 71 calories, 6.4g fat, 2.6g protein, 2.8 carbs, 1.6g fiber

Peanut Cream Cookies

Ingredients:

1/2 c. vanilla whey/
　　egg white protein
3/4 c. peanut flour
　　(or almond flour)
1/4 tsp baking soda
1/4 tsp Celtic sea salt
1/4 c. peanut butter
　　(or almond)
1/4 c. Just Like Sugar
　　(or erythritol)
1 tsp stevia glycerite
2 TBS water (to hold
　　dough together)

FILLING:
1/2 c. peanut butter
1/2 c. cream cheese
1/4 c. Just Like Sugar
1/2 tsp stevia glycerite

Directions...

Preheat the oven to 400 degrees F (200 degrees C). In a medium bowl, stir together the whey, peanut/almond flour, baking soda and salt. Cut in the peanut butter using a pastry blender or your fingers until the butter lumps are smaller than peas. Stir in the water and sweetener to form a stiff dough. On parchment paper, roll the dough out to 1/8 inch in thickness. On a cookie sheet, place 1/4 inch balls 2 inches apart. Flatten balls into circles (I used a measuring cup). Bake for 10-12 minutes in the preheated oven, until edges are lightly browned. Cool in oven to crisp up.

FILLING: Mix together and use to hold cookies together. (Dairy allergy: see pg. 9)

Makes 12 servings.
NUTRITIONAL COMPARISON (per serving)

Traditional Nutter Butter =
160 calories, 8g fat, 2g protein, 20 carbs, 1g fiber

"Healthified" Peanut Cream Cookies =
160 calories, 11g fat, 10.5g protein, 5 carbs, 2g fiber (3 effective carbs)

Ingredients:

1/2 c. vanilla whey/
  egg white protein
3/4 c.up peanut flour
  (or almond flour)
1/4 tsp baking soda
1/4 tsp Celtic sea salt
1/4 c. butter/coconut oil
1/4 c. erythritol
1 tsp stevia glycerite
4 TBS cocoa powder
2-4 TBS water (to hold
  dough together)

FILLING:

8 oz cream cheese
2 TBS unsweetened
  almond milk
4 TBS erythritol
1 tsp stevia glycerite

Directions...

Preheat the oven to 350 degrees F (200 degrees C). In a medium bowl, stir together the whey, peanut/almond flour, cocoa, baking soda and salt. Cut in the butter using a pastry blender or your fingers until the butter lumps are smaller than peas. Stir in the almond milk and sweetener to form a stiff dough. On a cookie sheet, place 1/4 inch balls 2 inches apart. Flatten balls into circles (I used a measuring cup). Bake for 10-12 minutes in the preheated oven, until edges are lightly browned. Cool in oven to crisp up.

FILLING: Mix all ingredients together and use to hold two chocolate cookies together. (Dairy allergy: see pg. 9)

Makes 12 servings.
NUTRITIONAL COMPARISON (per serving)

Traditional Oreo =
140 calories, 7g fat, 1g protein, 21 carbs, 0g fiber

"Healthified" Chocolate Cream Filled Cookie =
135 calories, 11g fat, 8g protein, 3 carbs, 1.1g fiber

Even though they claim, tran-fat free, this isn't true. Partially hydrogenated oils are listed in the ingredients. If you look closely the cookie photo says "per serving." If the total amount is less than 1 gram, they can claim this, but even 1 gram is enough to cause a snowball effect of issues. Not to mention it takes 9 months to detox our bodies from these plastic-like fats!

Are you eating a "clean" "fat-free" diet and losing your hair? Vitamins A, D, E and K are fat-soluble, meaning you can't absorb them without fat! Also, too often we grab "food" in lieu of healthy options, which eventually can create undesired issues in our body. We need these vitamins for proper functioning of our bodies and our brains.

DEFICIENCIES IN:

VITAMIN A = acne, dry skin and hair, itching eyes, often making sinus noises, and prone to catching the flu. Take 1 tsp Cod Liver Oil/day.

VITAMIN B = memory issues, confusion, bad breath, dark tongue, dry hair, rough skin, tender muscles, irritability.

VITAMIN C = bruising, muscle loss, bloody gums, cavities, and nosebleeds. Decreasing sugar is also important because sugar competes with Vitamin C to get into the cell and sugar always wins!

VITAMIN D = sensitivity to pain, Seasonal Effective Disorder, digestive issues, nervousness, pale skin. Increase sun exposure and high dose of Vitamin D.

VITAMIN E = losing hair at rapid rates, cataracts, and muscle weakness.

VITAMIN K = bruising and brittle bones.

FOLIC ACID = fatigue, depression/anxiety, sore tongue.

CALCIUM = brittle fingernails, eczema, tooth decay, and strange numbness and tingling in arms/legs

CHROMIUM = out of control blood sugar (jittery before lunch), lack of energy and excitement.

IRON = brittle nails, dry hair, pale skin, dizziness. This is a tricky one...eat more grass-fed red meat. If you are still low on iron, I would detect a food allergy causing you to not absorb iron. Do not take a supplement unless diagnosed with an iron deficiency; even then iron supplements are very poorly absorbed.

MAGNESIUM = chocolate cravings, urinary urgency, broken nails, nervousness, restless legs/twitching, sensitivity to noise.

POTASSIUM = bad hair and skin, water retention, edema.

SODIUM = confusion, dizziness, lethargy, and vomiting. Use quality Celtic Sea Salt.

ZINC = brittle nails, poor circulation, bruising, splitting hair, salty cravings.

FYI: Birth control pills deplete our cells of zinc and getting pregnant too soon before having healthy zinc levels can cause birth defects, such as cleft pallets. My suggestion is to take zinc for 6 months after going off birth control before trying to conceive.

Maria Emmerich

Coconut Fudge Rings

Ingredients:

COOKIES:

1 c. butter/coconut oil

1 c. Just Like Sugar

1/2 c. erythritol

2 tsp stevia glycerite

1 egg

1 1/2 c. blanched
    almond flour

1/2 c. coconut flour

1 tsp aluminum free
    baking powder

1 tsp Celtic sea salt

COCONUT CARAMEL:

See page 25.

1/2 c. unsweetened
    coconut flakes

CHOCOLATE DRIZZLE:

See page 25.

Directions: Preheat the oven to 325 degrees F. In

a medium bowl, cream the butter, Just Like Brown Sugar, erythritol
and stevia (add in egg if using). Cream for a few minutes until very
fluffy. In a separate bowl mix together the almond flour, coconut
flour, baking powder, and salt. Slowly add in the dry ingredients to the
wet and mix until smooth. In between 2 pieces of parchment (greased
parchment), roll the dough out into 1/4 in thick dough. Using circle
cut-outs, cut into Samoa cookie shapes. Place cookies about 2 inches
apart. Bake in preheated oven for 17-20 minutes or until golden around
the edges. Cool completely on the baking sheet before removing from
cookie sheet.

COCONUT CARAMEL: See page 25 for caramel. Stir in dried coconut
flakes to caramel sauce. Place 1-2 TBS of this mixture on top of each
circle. Set in freezer to set. Meanwhile make the chocolate sauce.

CHOCOLATE DRIZZLE: see page 25. Place 1/2 the chocolate in a
shallow bowl and dip the bottom of the cookies into the chocolate.
Place on parchment paper. Put the other 1/2 of the chocolate in a
small ziplock bag. Cut the corner of the bag and use to pipe stripes
over the cookies.

Makes 24 cookies.

NUTRITIONAL COMPARISON (per serving)

Traditional Cookie = 140 calories, 7g fat, 1g protein, 19 carbs, 1g fiber

"Healthified" Cookie = 125 calories, 11g fat, 3g protein, 5 carbs, 3.8g fiber

Fructose Facts

Agave Syrup is marketed as "low glycemic" and that is true, but let's look into why agave syrup is "low glycemic." It is due to the shockingly high concentration of fructose. It is 90% fructose and 10% glucose. Sugar is about 50/50% fructose to glucose, honey is about 55% fructose, high fructose corn syrup can range from 55-65% fructose.

WHY FRUCTOSE IS SO HARMFUL

1. Fructose can only be metabolized by the liver; glucose on the other hand can be metabolized by every cell in the body. Fructose raises triglycerides (blood fats) like no other food. Fructose bypasses the enzyme phosphofructokinase, which is the rate-limiting enzyme for glucose metabolism. Fructose is shunted past the sugar-regulating pathways and into the fat-formation pathway. The liver converts this fructose to fat, which, unfortunately, remains in the liver = FATTY LIVER DISEASE. Consuming fructose is essentially consuming fat! This is why I see so many children with fatty liver disease...they aren't drinking alcohol, they are drinking sodas, juices and consuming too much fructose!

2. Fructose reduces the sensitivity of insulin receptors, which causes type II diabetes. Insulin receptors are the way glucose enters a cell to be metabolized. Our cells become resistant to the effects of insulin and as a result, the body needs to make more insulin to handle the same amount of glucose. We also start to produce insulin as a defense mechanism even if we don't eat sugar or starch. YIKES! This is why we shouldn't allow our children to eat so much sugar and starch either; even if they are thin and active, you are setting them up for an adulthood where they can't enjoy a dessert without reaping the adverse effects.

3. Fructose is high in uric acid, which increases blood pressure and causes gout.

4. Fructose increases lactic acid in the blood. High levels cause metabolic acidosis especially for those with conditions such as diabetes.

5. Fructose accelerates oxidative damage and increases aging. Fructose changes the collagen of our skin making it prone to wrinkles.

6. High consumption of fructose leads to mineral losses: iron, calcium magnesium and zinc, which can lead to low bone density (osteoporosis). It also interferes with copper metabolism. This causes collagen and elastin being unable to form, which are connective tissue that hold the body together. A deficiency in copper can also lead to infertility, bone loss, anemia, defects of the arteries, infertility, high cholesterol levels, heart attacks and inability to control blood sugar.

7. Fructose has no effect on our hunger hormone (ghrelin) and interferes with brain's communication with leptin, which is the hormone that tells us to stop eating and you CAN become leptin resistant!

Ingredients:

1 zucchini or jicama

2 TBS coconut oil/ butter

3 TBS Just Like Brown Sugar

1 TBS lemon juice

2 tsp vanilla

1 tsp cinnamon

Directions: Peel the jicama or zucchini, cut
lengthwise into quarters (if using zucchini remove the seeds).
Slice into "apple" slices or cubes. Heat the butter over high
heat in a medium skillet. When the butter has melted and has
turned brown (not black). Stir in all the ingredients and cook
on medium heat until the veggie is to desired consistancy (the
longer you cook it the softer it will be). Adjust the sweetener
and cinnamon, if needed.

Makes 4 servings.
NUTRITIONAL COMPARISON (per serving)

Traditional Fried Apples =
111 calories, 5.9g fat, 0.2g protein, 14 carbs, 1g fiber

"Healthified" Fried Zucchini =
67 calories, 5.9g fat, 0.7g protein, 2.7 carbs, 1g fiber

"Healthified" Fried Jicama =
71 calories, 5.9g fat, 0.3g protein, 3.7 carbs, 1.8g fiber

VIACTIV Calcium Chew Ingredients:

Corn Syrup, Calcium Carbonate, Sugar, Nonfat Milk, Butter, Partially Hydrogenated Vegetable Oil (soybean and cottonseed), Soy Lecithin, Natural and Artificial Flavor, Glyceryl Monostearate, Carrageenan, Sodium Citrate, Sodium Phosphate, Vitamin D3, Vitamin K1

Calcium Facts

I am officially repulsed by our FDA! I knew that there would be corn syrup in these "so-called" healthy calcium supplements, but TRANS-FAT! How ridiculous! AND I didn't think that corn syrup would be the first ingredient ...no wonder they taste so good. Sugar upsets the calcium/phosphorus ratio in the blood more than any other single factor. It also stresses the adrenal glands and upsets the hormone balance which affects calcium metabolism.

The United States has some of the highest calcium intakes in the entire world, yet we have the highest rate of hip fractures! So why is this??? One reason is that it doesn't supply adequate magnesium. Studies of our ancestors' pre-agricultural diets indicate that magnesium was probably consumed at about a 1:1 ratio with calcium. But now, the Calcium-Magnesium ratio is 12:1 in dairy. Since calcium and magnesium compete for the same absorption mechanisms, the imbalanced intake associated with our modern diet may well lead to magnesium deficiency. One feature of magnesium deficiency is the inhibition of osteoblasts (the cells that build and maintain bones).

Calcium imbalance symptoms may include fatigue, depression, defensiveness, muscle weakness, pain, arteriosclerosis, arthritis, kidney stones and gallstones. Others are bone spurs, rigidity, slow metabolism, constipation, social withdrawal and spondylitis (rigidity and inflammation of the spine). Don't get me wrong, most people need more calcium, BUT we need quality calcium to get into our bones...not just poor quality supplements that are going to cause problems. We need more calcium due to the pasteurization of milk, and the consumption of grains, sugar, and other nutritional imbalances (such as low vitamin D levels and inadequate magnesium intake). In addition, impaired digestion, intestinal infections, and stress all reduce calcium absorption, digestion and utilization.

A diet high in phytic acid, which is found in the bran of whole grains, interferes with calcium absorption. This acid binds to a variety of minerals including calcium, to form insoluble salts, called phytates, which are wasted from the body. Since grains are a relatively new food, from an evolutionary perspective, it appears that we have not yet developed digestive tracts which can break down these phytates.

Some of my favorite calcium filled foods and recipes are:

1. KALE (I LOVE Kale Chips)
2. Cottage Cheese (my Protein Pancakes)
3. Cheddar cheese (my Cheez It Crackers)
4. Sesame seeds (my Salad Toppers)
5. Canned Salmon (my Salmon Patties)
6. Pecans/Walnuts/Brazil Nuts (my Pecan Sandies)
7. Cabbage (my Pasta)
8. Broccoli/spinach (my Loaded Broccoli)
9. Rhubarb (my Rhubarb Crisp)
10. Almonds, almond flour, almond milk (most of my recipes)
11. Brewer's yeast (my homemade "POPCORN")
12. Artichokes (Easy Pizza Casserole)
13. Shrimp (Seafood Chowder)
14. Sunflower Seeds (my Energy Bars)
15. Peanuts (my Reece's Mini Muffins)
16. Eggs (my Spice Cake and most recipes)

Additional awesome sources of Calcium = kelp, sardines with bones, bokchoy, watercress, parsley, ripe olives, romaine lettuce, pumpkin seeds, celery, and fish.

Are you grabbing Weight Watcher's Ice Cream off the shelf while trying to lose weight? THINK AGAIN!

Ingredients:

Milk Fat and Nonfat Milk, Sugar, Fudge Revel (Maltitol Syrup, Water, Maltitol, Cocoa Processed with Alkali, Butter, Nonfat Dry Milk, contains 2% or Less of: Pectin, Salt, Potassium Sorbate as Preservative, Sucralose) Peanut Butter Base (Peanuts, Peanut Oil, Salt, Mono and Diglycerides) Peanut Brittle (Peanuts, Sugar, Corn Syrup, Molasses, Butter, Sodium Bicarbonate, Salt, Vanilla) Polydextrose, Maltodextrin, Cellulose Gel, Mono & Diglycerides, Cellulose Gum, Carrageenan, Polysorbate 80, Vitamin A Palmitate.

You may think the key to weight loss is "Calories In, Calories Out"…It is WAY more complicated than that.

WHY TRANS-FATS ARE SO BAD? Well, for MANY reasons, but one thing is that it slows metabolism. The oils are most likely partially hydrogenated soybean oil. Soy blocks the absorption of zinc and iodine from the thyroid, which depresses the thyroid. A snowball effect happens: this will lower your energy levels, you don't feel like exercising, and your body can't process the food as efficiently and eventually makes you fatter!

In Gary Taubes book, <u>Why We Get Fat and What To Do About It</u>, a very interesting study conducted by the National Institute of Health, had 20,000 women who were very overweight go on a low calorie diet. On average, the women consumed 360 calories a day less on their diets than they did when they first agreed to participate. If obesity is caused by overeating, then these women were "under-eating" by 360 calories/day. They ate 20% less calories than what the public-health agencies tell us women should eat. The result? After 8 years, the women lost an average of 2 pounds each! AND their waist circumference increased! Which demonstrates that the women didn't lose fat, they lost muscle.

This is why a calorie isn't a calorie! A pound of fat contains 3500 calories. Eating 360 calories less everyday should have had the women lose 2 pounds of fat in the first 2 weeks and more than 36 pounds in the first year! It is all about WHAT we eat rather than how much. Our bodies create biological responses to everything we consume! Choosing the right foods at the right time is an art.

SPECIFIC INGREDIENTS: Making low sugar ice cream is tricky. If you use erythritol or ZSweet for a sweetener, it hardens to a ROCK! BUT if you use Chicory Root (AKA "Just Like Sugar") it stays nice and creamy! Another trick is to always add a pinch of salt to the mixture.

Ingredients:

5 egg yolks

1 c. Just Like Sugar

1 tsp stevia glycerite

1 c. heavy whipping cream

1 c. unsweetnened
   almond milk

1 tsp Celtic sea salt

PEANUT BUTTER SWIRL:

1/2 c. natural peanut butter

1/4 c. butter or coconut oil

1/4 c. erythritol

1/2 tsp stevia glycerite

1/4 c. unsweetened
   almond milk

CHOCOLATE SWIRL:
See page 25.
Swirl into finished ice cream.

Directions...

In a medium saucepan place the egg yolks and sweeteners in to mix on high with a hand mixer. Whip yolks until light in color and double in size. Stir in the whipping cream. Place the saucepan onto medium heat on the stove and cook, stirring constantly (I used my hand mixer). Stir until thickened into a custard. Remove from heat and stir in the almond milk and salt. Let cool completely (I cooled overnight...it was hard to wait!). Place into your ice cream machine and watch the magic happen within 45 minutes or according to your ice cream maker's directions. Freeze until set for vanilla ice cream or stir in your favorite swirl flavor to mix it up.
(Dairy allergy: see pg. 9)

Makes 5 servings.
NUTRITIONAL COMPARISON (per 1/2 cup serving)
Ben & Jerry's Vanilla = 230 calories, 32g fat, 4g protein, 23 carbs, 0g fiber,
"Healthified" Vanilla = 137 calories, 13g fat, 4g protein, 1.3 carbs, 0g fiber

Ingredients in store bought cake cone:

Enriched Wheat Flour (contains Niacin, Reduced Iron, Thiamine Mononitrate, Riboflavin, Folic Acid)Tapioca Flour, Sugar, Vegetable Oil Shortening (Partially Hydrogenated Soybean Oil, Partially Hydrogenated Canola Oil, and/ or Corn Oil) Leavening (Sodium Bicarbonate, Ammonium Bicarbonate) Salt, Natural Flavor, Annato (Vegetable Color)

ADHD

Next time you serve your kids an ice cream cone...remember this:

NO one wishes harm on their children, but if you feed them trans-fats, you are unknowingly setting them up for severe health issues. This is because trans-fats in foods are like BIG SUV's trying to park into a "compact" parking spaces of our cells that are reserved for healthy Omega 3 fats (DHA). When this happens, our neurotransmitters responsible for focus, mood, and memory have a hard time finding and recognizing their receptors due to the inflammation of the membranes on the brain cells caused by the consumption of trans fats.

Brain levels of the neurotransmitter dopamine (important for mood and focus) are lowered by 95% when you ingest trans fats. BUT what is even more disturbing, is that when you switch to eating 100% trans-fat free our brain remains unable to produce normal amounts of dopamine in the hippocampus (the part of the brain most responsible for consolidating memory). This is one reason for the high rates of ADHD and depression.

Children who start at age 3 or 4 eating a steady diet of fast food, pop tarts, commercially prepared fish sticks, stick margarine, cake, candy, cookies and microwave popcorn can be expected to have a harder time focusing, an increase risk of depression, have heart disease and strokes at earlier ages. BUT even if you avoid typical "junk food," you must remain a detective! I have seen trans-fats in refrigerated SALSA!

Maria Emmerich

Ice Cream Cone

Ingredients:

1 egg white, whipped

1 TBS butter or coconut oil (melted)

1/4 c. almond flour

1/4 c. vanilla whey/egg white protein

Directions... Heat a pizzelle
skillet on high. In a medium bowl, whip the egg white until very frothy. Add in the rest of the ingredients until smooth. Place 1 TBS dough onto greased skillet, close tightly. Let sit for 1-3 minutes depending on skillet directions. While you are removing, before it cools, roll into a cone shape.

Makes 8 cones.
NUTRITIONAL COMPARISON (per cone):

Traditional sugar CONE =
50 calories, 1g fat, 1g protein, 10 carbs, 0 fiber

"Healthified" Cone =
50 calories, 3g fat, 4g protein, 1.3 carbs, trace fiber

Smucker's Twix Magic Shell

Ingredients:

Sugar,
Sunflower Oil,
Coconut Oil,
Wheat Flour,
Cocoa, Chocolate,
Partially Hydrogenated Vegetable Oil (Soybean and Cottonseed Oils)
2% or Less of:
Artificial and Natural Flavors,
Salt, Soy Lecithin,
Cocoa Processed with Alkali,
Vanilla, Sodium Bicarbonate,
Vanillin (Artificial Flavor) Milk.

Trans-Fat and Pregnancy

When you or someone you know was pregnant, did they think they could eat whatever they wanted due to the fact that they were "Eating for 2?" Eating ice cream with a trans-fat filled cone dipped in chocolate is an equation for an unhealthy fetus.

Trans-fats cause extensive damage to a fetus, and most importantly, the brain of the developing fetus. Trans-fats are found in peanut butter, margarine, and almost every packaged food including Saltine crackers, Lipton Soup Mix....I've even found it in salsa! Trans-fatty acids are also called "hydrogenated oils" because the hydrogenation process is how they are created. The hydrogenation process changes the chemical structure of certain f ats and creates a monster of a molecule which can damage the brain of a fetus, cause cancer, cause Type 2 diabetes, and a whole host of other health problems.

Trans-fats have even been found in baby foods, such as infant cereal. When we eat trans fatty acids, they enter the "parking spots" of our cells reserved for essential fatty acids (EFAs) that are needed for brain development. Our brain is over 60% fat and when we fill it with trans fats instead of healthy DHA fats, our memory, learning and development is severely affected.

Even if you don't feed your baby and children these packaged foods, babies are still getting high doses of trans fats if the mother is eating it; trans fats pass through placenta to the fetus. Once born, the trans fat ingested by mothers is passed to their babies through breast milk. In fact, it has been proven that breast milk contains among the highest levels of trans fats reported. This IS NOT a time to eat whatever you want, you should be more concerned about what you are putting in your body at this time. I know that cravings strike and I am not saying never give into them, I'm just saying...try this recipe instead!

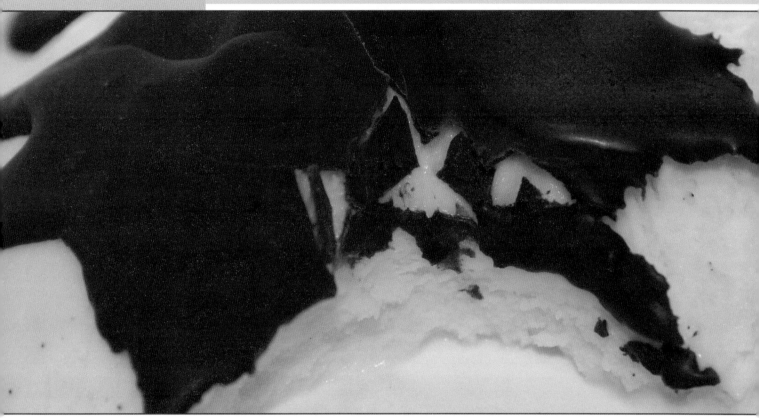

Ingredients:

6 TBS butter/coconut oil

6 TBS unsweetened
   cocoa powder

1/4 tsp stevia glycerite

4 TBS Just Like Sugar

1/2 tsp Celtic sea salt

Directions...

Melt coconut oil over low heat. Stir in chocolate, sweetener and salt until completely melted. Allow to cool to room temperature before drizzling over ice cream.

Makes 6 servings.
NUTRITIONAL COMPARISON (per serving)
Smucker's Shell = 210 calories, 15g fat, 1g protein, 18 carbs, trace fiber
"Healthified" Shell = 129 calories, 14g fat, 1g protein, 3 carbs, 1.6g fiber
(1.4 effective carbs)

ADDITIONAL FLAVOR IDEAS:

Peppermint Patty: 1 tsp mint oil
Almond Joy: 1 tsp almond oil
Creamsicle: 1 tsp orange oil and 1/2 tsp vanilla oil
Key Lime: 1 tsp lime oil
Twix: 1/2 tsp vanilla oil and chunks of "healthified" Twix
Snicker's: 1/2 tsp almond oil and 1/2 tsp vanilla oil AND "healthified" Snicker's.

Ingredients:

ICE CREAM LAYER:

1 c. whipping cream

8oz cream cheese

1/4 c. Just Like Sugar

1 tsp stevia glycerite

1/2 tsp Celtic sea salt

NUGGET LAYER:

1/4 c. butter/coconut oil

1/4 c. erythritol

1 tsp stevia glycerite

1/4 c. vanilla egg white/
   whey protein

8 oz cream cheese
   or coconut cream

1/2 c. natural peanut butter

1 tsp vanilla

1 c. salted peanuts, chopped

CHOCOLATE LAYER:

2 TBS butter/coconut oil

1 oz unsweetened
   baking chocolate

10 TBS heavy cream
   or coconut milk

1/2 c. *powdered erythritol

1 tsp stevia glycerite

Directions...

ICE CREAM LAYER: In a stand mixer or a large bowl, whip the cream. Add in the sweetener and softened cream cheese and salt (salt helps from hardening too much) until well combined. Line muffin tins with paper baking cups and place about 3-4 TBS into each liner. Chill in freezer while making Nugget Layer.

NUGGET LAYER: In a saucepan boil 1/4 cup of butter, sweetener, and 1/4 cup whey protein together for about 5 minutes. Take off stove and add 8 ounces cream cheese, 1/2 cup natural peanut butter, 1 tsp vanilla, and 1 cup peanuts. Pour over first layer that was chilling then place back in freezer.

CHOCOLATE LAYER: Place the erythritol in a coffee grinder and blend into a smooth powdered sugar texture (this is optional, but provides a smooth chocolate). Place the butter and chopped chocolate in a double boiler (or in a heat safe dish over a pot of boiling water). Stir well until just melted (don't burn the chocolate!), add in the cream and sweetener. Stir until smooth and thick Smooth over each ice cream bar. Place back in freezer to set.

Makes 16 servings.
NUTRITIONAL COMPARISON (per bar)

Traditional Snicker's Ice Cream Bar =
240 calories, 11g fat, 4g protein, 24 carbs, 1g fiber

"Healthified" Ice Cream Candy Bar =
250 calories, 24g fat, 8g protein, 4.5 carbs, 1.6g fiber

Milk Chocolate
(Sugar,
Cocoa Butter,
Chocolate,
Skim Milk,
Lactose,
Milkfat,
Soy Lecithin,
Artificial Flavor)
Peanuts,
Corn Syrup,
Milkfat,
Skim Milk,
Vegetable Oil
(Partially
Hydrogenated
Soybean and/or
Hydrogenated Palm
Kernel Oil),
Salt, Lactose,
Egg Whites,
Chocolate,
Artificial Flavor.

Partially hydrogenated oils don't just damage your cells, causing allergies, arthritis and auto immune diseases, but in they also make you fat!

Essential fatty acids are called 'essential' because your body NEEDS them and you can only get them through food. Your brain and body are very smart, even though your stomach may feel full, your brain never tells you to stop eating, because it still needs the essential fatty acids to sustain life. You will never be full until you do.

Partially hydrogenated oils make you gain weight because they interfere with the body's ability to ingest and utilize the healthy fats that you want to fill your cells with. Imagine this, your cells are like neat parking lots. When you eat omega 3 fats, they are like little Smart Cars that park nice and neat into the parking spots that feed our body by decreasing inflammation (everything from joint pain to asthma to heart disease). BUT when we eat trans fats they are like huge SUVs that don't fit into these parking spots, but they force their way in anyway....damaging the cars around them so they can't run anymore (or help our body) AND they cause our fat cells to grow! If you eat even more trans-fats, those SUVs get mad because they can't find a parking spot, so they just drive around furiously in your body and bounce into all the cells causing free-radicals. To read more on how to decrease free-radicals, check out the Supplement chapter in my book Secrets to a Healthy Metabolism.

Over time, more and more SUV are filling the parking spots which leaves no room for the Smart Cars. NOW new parking lots (fat cells) have to be built to make room for them. So now our body gets bigger, we have more inflammation and more health problems like asthma, arthritis, heart disease ...not a good outcome!

Ingredients:

CHOCOLATE COATING:
2 c. ChocoPerfection bars
1 c. Natural Peanut Butter

NUGGET LAYER:
1/4 c. butter
1/4 c. erythritol
1 tsp stevia glycerite
1/4 c. vanilla egg white/
   whey protein
1 c. cream cheese
1/4 c. natural peanut butter
1 tsp vanilla
1 1/2 c. salted peanuts,
   chopped

CARAMEL LAYER:
see page 25.

Directions...

In a saucepan melt 2 cup of the chocolate and 1 cup of creamy peanut butter. Spread HALF on bottom of cake pan. Then put in freezer to set up while next layer is prepared.

NUGGET LAYER: In a saucepan boil 1/4 cup of butter, 1/4 cup of erythritol, 1 tsp stevia glycerite, and 1/4 cup whey protein together for about 5 minutes. Take off stove and add 1 cup cream cheese, 1/4 cup peanut butter, 1 tsp vanilla, and 1 1/2 cups peanuts. Pour over first layer that was chilling then place back in freezer. (Dairy allergy: see pg. 9)

CARAMEL LAYER: See page 25. Spread over the top of the second layer that is chilling. Place back in freezer. Next you will want to cut into candy bar shapes...I like to make them "mini" for portion control. Warm the chocolate coating and roll the frozen bars in the chocolate to coat well. Place on parchment paper and chill.

Makes 24 candybars.
NUTRITIONAL COMPARISON (per bar)
Traditional Snickers = 271 calories, 14g fat, 4.3g protein, 34.5 carbs, 1.3g fiber
"Healthified" Candy Bar = 254 calories, 19g fat, 10g protein, 8 carbs, 4.6g fiber

Ingredients in Paydays:

TBHQ

Peanuts,
Sugar,
Corn Syrup,
Partially
Hydrogenated
Vegetable Oil
(contains Soybean and
Cottonseed Oils)
Nonfat Milk, Salt,
Mono- and
Diglycerides,
Egg Whites,
TBHQ,
Soy Protein,
and Citric Acid

Candy bars were one of my weaknesses in my past life. But now with understanding on what certain chemicals do to our cells and brain, I have no problem walking by them in the grocery store. Instead, I enjoy every bite of my homemade eggs without any guilt.

TBHQ comes from petroleum (think "lighter fluid"). It is applied either to the carton of fast food items or sprayed directly onto them, as well as in various other prepackaged food items. TBHQ is banned in other countries. TBHQ keeps fats from going rancid, so you see it in a lot of foods that they want to have a long shelf life. It is considered an "anti-oxidant" BUT it can itself be oxidized into harmful molecules, like tert-butylquinone...causing a TIRED TOXIC LIVER (see pg. 56).

But it also promotes production of quinonereductase, which is linked to cancer. TBHQ can cause a full range of reactions from asthma to anxiety, ADHD, insomnia, depression, tiredness, learning difficulties and children's behavior problems. This chemical is also found to effect estrogen levels...are you trying to get pregnant? Suffering from menopausal symptoms? I would avoid this like the plague.

In pre-packaged foods, if you see the words "no trans-fats," look for TBHQ in the ingredient lists. Some manufacturer's, such as Kellogg's, are using this "trickery," and are using TBHQ instead of trans-fats. Is it better than trans-fat? No. BUT what is even scarier... if you don't see it, that does not mean it is not there. Manufacturers are not required to list "secondary" ingredients. If you don't believe me, call the company and ask if their oil now contains TBHQ. Thank you FDA!

Oh, AND always make sure you use NATURAL peanut butter...Jiff has trans-fats!

Maria Emmerich

Peanut Candy Bar

Ingredients:

CARAMEL LAYER:
See page 25.

NUGGET LAYER:
1/4 c. butter

1/4 c. erythritol

1 tsp stevia glycerite

1/4 c. vanilla egg white/
    whey protein

1 c. cream cheese

1/4 c. peanut butter

1 tsp vanilla

1 1/2 c. salted peanuts,
    chopped

Directions...

CARAMEL LAYER: See page 25 for directions. Place 2 TBS of cooled caramel in each slot of an ice cube tray lined with foil or plastic wrap (so you can remove it easily) and freeze.

NUGGET LAYER: In a saucepan boil 1/4 cup of butter, 1/4 cup of erythritol, and 1 tsp stevia glycerite, and 1/4 cup whey protein together for about 5 minutes. Take off stove and add 1 cup cream cheese, 1/4 cup creamy natural peanut butter, and 1 tsp vanilla. Cool slightly. Remove the caramels from the ice cube trays. Using your hands, form a layer of nugget around the caramel. Then roll the candy bar in salted peanuts. Place in the fridge to 'set' for at least 60 minutes. (Dairy allergy: see pg. 9)

Makes 16 bars.
NUTRITIONAL COMPARISON (per bar)
Hershey's Payday = 240 calories, 12g fat, 7g protein, 27 carbs, 2g fiber
"Healthified" Bar = 240 calories, 15g fat, 7g protein, 3.5 carbs, 1.2g fiber
            (MORE IMPORTANTLY...NO TRANS-FATS!)

Immune Health

Ingredients in a Traditional TWIX:

Milk Chocolate (Sugar, Cocoa Butter, Milk Ingredients, Cocoa Mass, Lactose, Soy Lecithin, Polyglycerol Polyricinoleate, Artificial Flavour) Enriched Flour (Flour, Niacin, Reduced Iron, Thiamine Mononitrate, Riboflavin, Folic Acid) Sugar, Hydrolyzed Palm and Palm Kernel Oil, Corn Syrup, Milk Ingredients, Dextrose, Salt, Cocoa Mass, Sodium Bicarbonate, Soy Lecithin, Soybean Oil, Artificial Flavor.

Have you ever noticed our kids get sick a lot from Halloween until Valentine's Day? HMMMM, there are a lot of Holidays in between that time that focus on candy. Sugar depresses the immune system. Vitamin C is needed by white blood cells so that they can phagocytize viruses and bacteria. White blood cells require a 50 times higher concentration inside the cell as outside so they have to accumulate vitamin C.

There is something called a "phagocytic index" which tells you how rapidly a particular lymphocyte can gobble up a virus, bacteria, or cancer cell. In 1970, Linus Pauling, discovered that white blood cells need a high dose of vitamin C and that is when he came up with his theory that you need high doses of vitamin C to combat the common cold. We know that glucose and vitamin C have similar chemical structures, so what happens when the sugar levels go up? They compete for one another when entering the cells. And the thing that mediates the entry of glucose into the cells is the same thing that mediates the entry of vitamin C into the cells. If there is more glucose around, there is going to be less vitamin C allowed into the cell. It doesn't take much: a blood sugar value of 120 reduces the phagocytic index by 75%. So when you eat sugar, think of your immune system slowing down to a crawl.

Simple sugars aggravate asthma, cause mood swings, magnify personality changes, muster mental illness, fuel nervous disorders, increase diabetes and heart disease, grow gallstones, accelerate hypertension, and magnify arthritis. Since sugar lacks minerals and vitamins, they draw upon the body's micro-nutrient stores in order to be metabolized into the system.

So what are you sending your kids off to school with? A bowl of cereal and skim milk? A Poptart? To keep your kids healthy and focused at school, try organic eggs with lots of omega 3's and healthy protein, or a Jay Rob whey protein shake. A protein filled breakfast is proven to increase focus and success in children as well as adults.

Ingredients:

1/2 c. vanilla whey/
    egg white protein

3/4 c. almond flour

1/4 tsp baking soda

1/4 tsp Celtic sea salt

1/4 c. butter or coconut oil

4 TBS erythritol

1/2 tsp stevia glycerite

1-2 TBS water

PEANUT BUTTER LAYER:

6 TBS natural peanut butter

6 TBS unsweetened almond milk

Stevia glycerite to taste

CHOCOLATE: See page 25.

Directions:

Preheat the oven to 375 degrees F. In a medium bowl, stir together the whey, almond flour, baking soda and salt. Cut in the butter using a pastry blender or your fingers until the butter lumps are smaller than peas. Stir in the water and sweetener to form a stiff dough. Take about 2 TBS of dough at a time to roll out long biscuit shapes. Place on cookie sheet. Bake for 7 minutes, turn off oven. Leave in oven for 3 more minutes to cool to crisp up. Place in freezer to freeze.

PEANUT BUTTER LAYER: Place all ingredients in a mixing bowl and stir until well combined. Add sweetener to taste. Place peanut butter sauce on top of the cookie and place in freezer to set.

CHOCOLATE LAYER: See page 25. Drizzle over the peanut butter covered cookie. Place in freezer to set.

Makes 12 bars.
NUTRITIONAL COMPARISON (per 2 Twix bars)
Traditional PB Twix = 290 calories, 14g fat, 2.8g protein, 37 carbs, 1g fiber
"Healthified" Bar = 195 calories, 15g fat, 8g protein, 4 carbs, 1.9g fiber
(2.1 effective carbs)

Fructose is a better energy source than other sugars because it causes a lower insulin response than glucose.

Fact:

Far from improving performance, eating fructose has been shown to harm performance. Your body stores twice as much muscle glycogen after eating glucose or sucrose than from eating fructose. It is also likely to cause gastrointestinal distress, even in small amounts.

Agave = 90% fructose!

Honey = 55% fructose

Pre-Race Fuel

Are you an athlete looking for a healthy energy idea and can't find one without junk? Here is a therapeutic snack filled with coconut to decrease inflammation in your joints! One of the reasons inflammation occurs is from a rapid rise in blood sugar, which causes biochemical changes in the cell. Staying away from sugar and high-glycemic (simple) carbohydrates, which the body rapidly converts to sugar, is one of the best ways to decrease inflammation. Athletes make the common mistake of relying on carbs and sugar for their fuel source. These are my athletes that "hit the wall." We can only store so much glucose in our liver and muscles; when that runs out, we need an additional fuel source. Consuming bananas and gel packs actually hinder performance. Fructose isn't absorbed in the small intestine and can cause GI distress.

Coconut is made up of Medium Chained Fatty Acid (MCFA). One of the most outstanding benefits of consuming MCFA's is that they do not require the liver and gallbladder to digest and emulsify them. For anyone with impaired fat digestion or a removed gallbladder, coconut oil is the only oil to consume as it is very easily digested.

By bypassing the liver and gallbladder, coconut oil creates instant energy and increased thermogenesis (increased metabolic rate in the body) which leads to more heat production as well as improved circulation. Improved circulation helps with energy because as we inhale oxygen it is carried via the hemoglobin to the mitochondria of our cells. The mitochondria are the 'powerhouse' part of our cell that burns fat and creates energy.

MCFA's are also known for having antimicrobial and anti-fungal properties, so they are beneficial to our immune system. In addition, coconut oil assists people with under-active thyroids by increasing the metabolic rate of the body and creating more energy.

Ingredients:

2 TBS coconut oil (melted)

2 TBS unsweetened
    cocoa powder

1 TBS almond butter

1 TBS coconut flour

Stevia glycerite (to taste)

Directions:

Mix cocoa into the coconut oil. Then add in the almond butter, mix until smooth. Then add the coconut flour (and sweetener if desired). Pour into mini ice cube trays. Freeze at least 5-6 minutes and either store in the fridge or freezer.

Makes 2 servings.

NUTRITIONAL COMPARISON (per serving)

Traditional Almond Joys =
235 calories, 13g fat, 2g protein, 29.2 carbs, 2.5g fiber

"Healthified" Almond Chocolates =
200 calories, 19g fat, 3g protein, 6 carbs, 3.3g fiber

Depression

Sugar, High
Fructose Corn
Syrup, Crisp
Rice, Partially
Hydrogenated
Vegetable Oil
(Palm Kernel
and Soybean
Oil), Vegetable
Oil (Cocoa
Butter, Palm,
Shea, Sunflower
and/or Safflower
Oil), Partially
Defatted Peanuts,
Nonfat Milk,
Chocolate, Partially
Hydrogenated
Coconut Oil,
Corn Syrup Solids,
Whey, Contains
2% or Less of:
Dairy Butter,
Milk Fat, Salt,
Mono- and
Diglycerides,
Soy Lecithin,
Molasses, Barley
Malt, Vanillin
(Artificial Flavor),
Disodium Phosphate.

Are you feeling a little "down in the dumps?" or not as "happy-go-lucky" as you once were? What types of foods are you putting in your mouth? Even if you are good 80% of the time and the other 20% you let loose with your diet, you may be filling your cells with trans-fat and those detrimental fats take 9 MONTHS to detox from our body! About 60% of clients that I see are taking a prescription drug for depression or anxiety. Could our food supply be affecting our brain health? I KNOW so! It is not your fault for these low moods. We just need to start eating quality "food" rather than fill our stomach with "substance."

Certain foods make us feel better by boosting brain neurotransmitter levels such as serotonin and dopamine, and some foods make us feel terrible, one of which is trans fats. Trans fatty acids lead to biological changes that are linked not only to heart disease, but also to depression. Trans fats have a HUGE impact on LDL (bad) cholesterol which blocks blood flow to the brain. In the brain, substances secreted by inflammation interferes with neurotransmitters that affect mood.

When we consume even 1 gram of trans-fat, that plastic molecule finds our way to our cells and takes up the "parking" spot in our cells that were meant for healthy Omega 3 fats. The membranes of our neurons (the specialized brain cells that communicate with each other) are composed of a thin double-layer of fatty acid molecules. The myelin (the protective sheath that covers communicating neurons) is composed of 30% protein and 70% fat. One of the most common fatty acids in myelin is oleic acid, which is also the most abundant fatty acid in human breast milk and in other foods like coconut milk, coconut oil as well as the oils from almonds, peanuts, pecans, macadamias, and avocados.

When we consume trans-fats instead of healthy omega fats filled with oleic acids, our cells no longer communicate and "Happy Cells are Talking Cells." The increase in depression in North America is in direct correlation with the decline in consumption of omega 3 fatty acids.

mE
Maria Emmerich

"Healthy" Chamacallit

Ingredients:

**PEANUT BUTTER
CRISPY CENTER:**

3/4 c. erythritol

1/2 tsp stevia glycerite

1/2 c. butter/coconut oil

1/2 c. natural
   peanut butter

3 c. whey crisps

CARAMEL LAYER:

See page 25.

CHOCOLATE LAYER:

See page 25.

Directions...

Combine the first 4 ingredients in a saucepan and warm until melted and mixed well. Add the whey crisps and mix. Form tin foil into candy bar shapes. Pour batter into the tinfoil shape. Let cool in fridge or freezer until set.

CARAMEL LAYER: See page 25. Add a layer of 1 TBS caramel on top of the whey crisp mold. Set in freezer to set up.

CHOCOLATE LAYER: See page 25. Once the caramel covered bars are cool, cover the bars in chocolate sauce and place back in the freezer to set.

Makes 12 servings.
NUTRITIONAL COMPARISON (per serving)
Whatchamacallit = 222 calories, 10g fat, 3.6g protein, 28.5 carbs, 0.9g fiber
"Healthy" Chamacallit = 210 calories, 12g fat, 7g protein, 3.8 carbs, 1.5g fiber

Steer Clear

Ingredients in 100 Grand:

Milk Chocolate (Sugar, Cocoa Butter, Chocolate, Nonfat Milk, Lactose, Milkfat, Soy Lecithin, Vanillin - an Artificial Flavor) Corn Syrup, Sugar, High Fructose Corn Syrup, Nonfat Milk, Crisped Rice (Rice Flour, Sugar, Salt, Barley, Malt, traces of Wheat Gluten) Coconut Oil, Butter, Mono- and Diglycerides, Salt, Soy Lecithin, Artificial and Natural Flavor.

ALZHEIMER'S Facts

So, what is wrong with grabbing a "treat" once in a while? Well, first off, 'once in awhile' triggers a snowball effect of cravings. Once you throw off your brain chemistry with high blood sugar levels the roller-coaster of brain imbalances begin. That is why I don't want anyone to think that they don't have the will-power for eating the "healthified" way! It isn't your fault that cravings happen! You can correct this with specific supplements and eating patterns to control insulin levels. Insulin is a powerful hormone that controls everything from cravings to brain chemistry and wrinkles!

One of the causes of brain aging is the decreased ability to metabolize glucose for brain conversion; to put it simpler....our cells can't process as many sugars and carbohydrates (this includes complex carbs, whole grains, and natural sweeteners like honey). In the past a candy bar was a rare treat, but now, we start the day with a bowl of cereal (Grapenuts = 23 tsp of sugar), which sets us up for sugar cravings at 3pm...hence the candy bar cravings! The daily blood sugar fluctuations cause impairment of glucose metabolism and combined with cell damage leads to dementia.

If you grew up on cereal for breakfast, peanut butter and jelly sandwiches for lunch and butter noodles for dinner, this creates an adulthood of insulin sensitivity that can lead to carbohydrate sensitivity and early biological aging. High carbohydrate foods literally age brains at early ages. This is because carbs and sugar increase inflammation and damaged cells occur on the inside of the body and brain. Okay, maybe you can't relate to brain issues yet, so here .... this inflammation decreases our skin's elasticity and collagen production which increases aging skin and premature wrinkles.

Ingredients:

CARAMEL LAYER:
See page 25.

**CHOCOLATE
CRISP LAYER:**
2 TBS butter/coconut oil

1 oz unsweetened
   baking chocolate

10 TBS heavy cream
   or coconut cream

1/4 c.up erythritol

1 tsp stevia glycerite

1 1/2 c. Chocolate
   Whey Crisps OR
   crushed macadamia nuts

Directions...

CARAMEL LAYER: See page 25 for directions. Place 2 TBS of caramel in each slot of an ice cube tray (lined with foil or plastic wrap so you can remove it easily) and freeze.

CHOCOLATE CRISP LAYER: Place the butter and chopped chocolate in a double boiler (or in a heat safe dish over a pot of boiling water...see photo). Stir well until just melted (don't burn the chocolate!), add in the cream, and sweetener. Stir until smooth and thick. Then add the whey crisps. Remove the caramels from the ice cube trays (twist the tray as if you had ice cubes in it). Dip each caramel into the chocolate to coat completely and then place on waxed paper. Cool until firm in the refrigerator, 1 to 2 hours.

Makes 16 candy bars.
NUTRITIONAL COMPARISON (per 1 mini candy bar)
Nestle 100 Grand = 180 calories, 8g fat, 1g protein, 29 carbs, 0g fiber
"Healthified" Bar = 165 calories, 12g fat, 6.3g protein, 3.6 effective carbs, 0g fiber

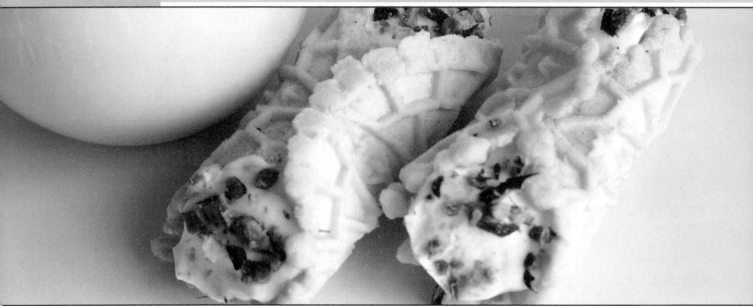

Ingredients:

SHELL:

1 egg white

1 TBS butter (melted)

1 oz cream cheese (soft)

1/4 c. almond flour

1/4 c. vanilla egg white/
   whey protein

FILLING:

3/4 c. whole milk ricotta
   cheese (drained overnight w/
   cheesecloth & squeezed dry)

3/4 c. mascarpone cheese
   (or cream cheese)

1/4 c. Truvia
   (or stevia glycerite to taste)

1/2 tsp vanilla

1/2 tsp ground cinnamon

A pinch of salt

Directions: Heat a pizzelle skillet on high.

Whip the white until frothy, not stiff. Add the almond flour, vanilla whey and other ingredients. Mix until smooth. Place 1 TBS dough onto greased skillet, close tightly. Let sit for 1-3 minutes depending on skillet directions. While you are removing, before it cools, roll into a cylinder shape. Set aside to cool. Mix filling ingredients together. Cover and refrigerate until ready to use (at least a couple of hours). Use a ziploc (cut the corner) and pipe into the shells. Let the filling smoosh out of each end of the shells, just a tad. Keep the cannoli refrigerated until dessert time or whenever you are ready to serve. (Dairy allergy: see pg. 9)

Makes 12 servings.
NUTRITIONAL COMPARISON: (per cannoli)

Traditional Cannoli =
250 calories, 7g fat, 4g protein, 44 carbs, trace fiber

"Healthified" Cannoli =
118 calories, 8g fat, 8.4g protein, 1.6 carbs, trace fiber

Peppermint Melts

Ingredients:

6 TBS coconut oil

1/3 c. coconut milk
(full fat)

1/3 c. Just Like Sugar
(or erythritol)

1/2 tsp stevia glycerite

1 TBS coconut flour

1 1/2 tsp mint extract,
divided

1/4 tsp Celtic sea salt

2 (2 oz) ChocoPerfection
Bars, chopped

2 TBS unsweetened
almond milk

Directions: Line small muffin pan with pieces

of muffin liners. In a medium bowl, mix together the coconut oil, 1/3 cup coconut milk, sweetener, coconut flour, 1 tsp mint and salt. Mix until you make a paste. Place the mixture into the prepared muffin pan. Place in freezer until frozen. Melt chocolate, 2 TBS almond milk, and 1/2 tsp mint and stir until smooth. Dip cooled/frozen coconut mixtures into chocolate, return to wax paper, and place in freezer to set. ENJOY!

NOTE: They melt fast so I recommend keeping them in the freezer.

Makes 12 servings.
NUTRITIONAL COMPARISON (per serving)

Traditional Peppermint Patty =
165 calories, 3g fat, 0g protein, 33 carbs, 0.9g fiber

"Healthified" Peppermint Melt =
99 calories, 9g fat, 0.3g protein, 3 carbs, 2.4g fiber

Maria Emmerich

Turtle Cheesecake

Ingredients:

CRUST:
1/2 c. coconut oil/butter

1 egg

1/2 c. Just Like Sugar

1/4 c. erythritol

1 tsp stevia glycerite

3/4 c. blanched
   almond flour

1/4 c. coconut flour

1/2 tsp baking powder

1 tsp Celtic sea salt

FILLING:
5 (8 oz) packages
   cream cheese

1 1/2 c. powdered*
   erythritol

1 tsp stevia glycerite

3/4 c. unsweetened
   almond milk

3 eggs

1 TBS vanilla extract

*Powdered erythritol will create a smoother texture. All you have to do is grind a bunch in a coffee grinder and keep it handy for recipes.

Directions...

Preheat the oven to 325 degrees F. In a medium bowl, cream the butter, egg, Just Like Brown Sugar, erythritol and stevia. Cream for a few minutes until very fluffy. In a separate bowl mix together the almond flour, coconut flour, baking powder, and salt. Slowly add in the dry ingredients to the wet and mix until smooth. This will be a thick pie dough, press onto bottom of springform pan. Place in oven to pre-bake the crust. Bake for 15 minutes or until lightly golden brown. Remove from oven and set aside to cool. In a large bowl, mix cream cheese with sweeteners until smooth. Blend in almond milk, and then mix in the eggs one at a time, mixing just enough to incorporate. Mix in vanilla until smooth. Pour filling into prepared crust. Bake in preheated oven for 1 hour. Turn the oven off, and let cake cool in oven with the door closed for 5 to 6 hours; this prevents cracking. Chill in refrigerator until serving. Meanwhile, make the caramel sauce and chocolate sauce.

CHOCOLATE SAUCE: See page 25. Top Cheesecake with sauce.

CARAMEL SAUCE: See page 25. Use to drizzle all over the cheesecake just before serving. You can also top with pecans.

Makes 12 servings.
NUTRITIONAL COMPARISON (per serving)

Tradiditonal Turtle Cheesecake =
760 calories, 47g fat, 4g protein, 53 carbs, 0.5g fiber (52.5 effective carbs)

"Healthified" Turtle Cheesecake =
487calories, 47g fat, 11g protein, 5.6 carbs, 1.6g fiber

mE

Muscle Tip

Alcohol and Our Body

Drinking alcohol is the most efficient way to slash your testosterone levels; women…we don't want this to happen either. Just a single event of serious drinking raises levels of the muscle-wasting stress hormone called cortisol and decreases the levels of testosterone for up to 24 hours. If you are working out to build strong fat burning muscles yet consuming alcohol, this actually breaks down muscle further and you end up with a slower metabolism because you break down muscle as you lift weights and you repair them as you rest if you have proper hormone levels.

When people go on a diet, they often choose the "light" version of their favorite alcoholic beverages in order to save a few calories. However, that is only a small piece of the puzzle. Fat metabolism is reduced by as much as 73% after only two alcoholic beverages. This scary fact shows that the primary effect of alcohol on the body is not so much how many calories we consume, but how it stops the body's ability to use your fat stores for energy.

Alcohol in the body is converted into a substance called acetate. Unlike a car that uses one supply of fuel, the body is able to draw from carbohydrates, fats and proteins for energy. When your blood acetate levels increase, your body uses acetate instead of fat. To make matters worse, the more you drink the more you tend to eat; and unfortunately, drinking will make your liver work to convert the alcohol into acetate, which means that the foods you consume at this time will be converted into extra fat on your body.

If that didn't sound bad enough; alcohol stimulates appetite and decreases your testosterone levels for up to 24 hours and increases estrogen by 300%. The infamous "beer belly" is really just an "estrogen belly." Biochemically, the higher your level of estrogen is, the more readily you absorb alcohol, but the slower you break it down.

Also, we all know that alcohol dehydrates us. In order for fat to be metabolized, it must first be released from the fat cell and then be transported by the bloodstream where it is pushed to the liver to be used as fuel. If you are dehydrated, the liver has to come to the aid of the kidneys and can't focus on its role of releasing fat.

Alcohol also affects every organ of the body, it's most dramatic impact is upon the liver. The liver cells normally prefer fatty acids as fuel, and package excess fatty acids as triglycerides, which they then route to other tissues of the body. However, when alcohol is present, the liver cells are forced to first metabolize the alcohol, letting the fatty acids accumulate in huge amounts. Alcohol metabolism permanently changes liver cell structure, which impairs the liver's ability to metabolize fats, which causes fatty liver disease.

Maria Emmerich

Ingredients:

LADY FINGERS:

5 egg whites

1 tsp cream of tartar

1/2 c. vanilla whey/
egg white protein

1 tsp stevia glycerite

FILLING:

6 egg yolks

1 1/4 cups erythritol

1 tsp stevia glycerite

1 1/4 c. mascarpone cheese

1 3/4 c. heavy
whipping cream

1/3 c. coffee
(sweetened to taste)

TOPPING:

1 tsp unsweetened
cocoa powder

Directions:

Preheat oven to 325 degrees F. In a clean, dry bowl, whip the whites and cream of tartar until stiff peaks form. Gently add in the protein powder and sweetener. Place the dough in a 9x9 in grease baking pan. Bake for 30-35 minutes or until light golden brown. Remove from oven and set aside.

FILLING: Combine egg yolks and sweetener in the top of a double boiler, over boiling water. Reduce heat to low, and cook for about 10 minutes, stirring constantly. Remove from heat and whip yolks until thick and lemon colored. Add mascarpone to whipped yolks. Beat until combined. In a separate bowl, whip cream to stiff peaks. Gently fold into yolk mixture and set aside. Cut the lady finger dough into 2 inch "fingers" and line the bottom and sides of a large glass bowl. Brush with coffee. Spoon half of the cream filling over the lady fingers. Repeat ladyfingers, coffee and filling layers. Garnish with cocoa. Refrigerate several hours or overnight. (Dairy allergy: see pg. 9)

Makes 12 servings.

NUTRITIONAL COMPARISON (per serving)
Traditional Tiramisu = 568 calories, 32g fat, 9.8g protein, 60 carbs, 0.8g fiber
"Healthified" Tiramisu = 159 calories, 12g fat, 10g protein, 2.2 carbs, trace fiber

Menopause Facts

Did you know… it takes your body 300 calories a day to ovulate? When our bodies stop ovulating, we stop burning an extra 300 calories per day. That equals to be 10 pounds per year! So, what do we need to do to change that? The science of menopausal metabolism points to two major hormones, estrogen and progesterone. Many menopausal women have excess estrogen and a deficiency of progesterone. Estrogen is the hormone that gives women ample curves, attractive breasts and youthful skin. However, too much estrogen causes too many curves—or you might say, bulges. Farmers have known this for years. They use a little synthetic estrogen to fatten their cattle. But women say to themselves: "I don't take any form of estrogen. Why do I have too much?" The sad truth is that estrogen comes from our food choices. Our bodies make more estrogen when we eat too many processed carbohydrates. Insulin, the master hormone, is secreted from the pancreas in response to sugar and processed carbohydrates. Insulin stores fat and also causes our bodies to make more estrogen. This link to extra estrogen is also connected to Polycystic Ovarian Syndrome; which can cause fertility issues in young women.

The banana, cereal and glass of juice that once worked for breakfast is now too high in sugar and it creates an insulin response. Insulin produces more estrogen, which creates more fat cells, which make more estrogen that creates more fat cells. So, your waist size increases, and your clothes are too tight! At this time in life, you need to reduce the processed carbohydrates, which will reduce the amount of glucose in your blood. With balanced blood sugar levels, less insulin is needed and less body fat is created. For better metabolism at menopause, eat less cereal, pasta, bread and sodas. Instead, start eating more vegetables, healthy fats, and real protein.

Unless the meat you eat is labeled "no hormones added," you are probably eating meat with added hormones. Many commercial farmers of beef and sheep use hormones to promote rapid weight gain in their animals. The best choice is organic, grass-fed meat which contains CLA (conjugated linoleic acid). Grass-fed animals have twice as much CLA as animals fed grains, and numerous studies have shown that CLA promotes healthy metabolism.

Weight gain or mood swings might be the result of an insulin response or poor food choices, but there are other possible causes. Lack of sleep, too much stress, insufficient progesterone, adrenal exhaustion, and inflammation all may contribute to your menopausal issues. Interestingly, all these factors have a nutrition connection.

So, if you need to indulge, try this treat that will keep your blood sugar under control. No hot flash side effects with this dessert!

Ingredients:

1 c. erythritol

1 tsp stevia glycerite

5 egg yolks

5 egg whites

1/3 c. unsweetened
   almond milk

1 tsp vanilla extract

1 c. blanched almond flour

1 1/2 tsp aluminum free
   baking powder

LECHES:

1 (14 ounce) can coconut milk

1/2 c. unsweetened
   almond milk

1 pint heavy whipping cream
   OR coconut cream

1 tsp stevia glycerite (or to taste)

Directions:

Preheat oven to 350 degrees F (175 degrees C). Grease bottom of a 9 inch spring form pan with coconut oil spray. Beat the egg yolks with erythritol until light in color and doubled in volume. Stir in almond milk, vanilla, almond flour, stevia and baking powder. In a separate bowl, beat egg whites until soft peaks form. Fold egg whites into yolk mixture. Pour into prepared pan. Bake at 350 degrees F (175 degrees C) for 45 to 50 minutes or until cake tester inserted into the middle comes out clean. Loosen edge of cake with knife before removing side of pan. Cool cake completely; place on a deep serving plate.

LECHES: Mix together coconut milk, 1 tsp stevia, almond milk and 1/4 cup of the whipping cream. Discard 1 cup of the measured milk mixture or cover and refrigerate. Pour remaining milk mixture over cake slowly until absorbed. Whip the remaining whipping cream until it thickens and reaches spreading consistency. Frost cake with whipped cream.

Makes 12 servings.

NUTRITIONAL COMPARISON (per serving)

Traditional TresLeches = 579 calories, 31g fat, 2g protein, 70.3 carbs, 0.4 g fiber

"Healthified" TresLeches = 303 calories, 29g fat, 6.3g protein. 5.5 carbs, 1.8g fiber

Fructose Facts

Dietary fructose is present primarily in sugar, high fructose corn syrup, honey, agave and fruit. Americans most frequently ingest fructose from sucrose (table sugar), which is 50% fructose and 50% glucose bonded together, high fructose corn syrup (HFCS) is about 55% fructose, honey is also 55% fructose. Agave, while 'natural' 90% fructose...NOT a health food! The average American in 1960 consumed 2 tsp of sugar/day. In 2011 it is over 65 tsp every day! Fructose consumption accounts for approximately 10.2% of total calories, EMPTY calories I might add. No wonder we have a problem with the rise in cancer, diabetes, liver disease, obesity....

All sugars can be made into triglycerides, a form of body fat; however, once you start the process of fat synthesis from fructose, it's hard to stop it. Our liver is like a 'traffic cop' that coordinates what we eat including sugars. It turns sugars into energy (if you are active), triglycerides, and cholesterol. Triglycerides are mainly formed in the liver. It is the liver's job, when it encounters glucose, to decide whether the body needs to store the glucose as glycogen, burn it for energy or turn the glucose into triglycerides. Even if you are an athlete, burning sugar for energy is an inefficient and limiting source of energy. This is why marathon runners "Hit the Wall." Your liver can only store 60-90 grams of carbs at a time. If you are an athlete and need more help on getting passed the 'wall' contact me for a consult on better energy sources!

Fructose, on the other hand, enters this metabolic pathway downstream, bypassing the 'traffic cop' and flooding the metabolic pathway. It basically sneaks into the rock concert without a ticket. This 'dumping of fructose' contributes to lots of triglyceride synthesis. So, in the end fructose gets made into fat VERY easily! This also causes 'fatty liver disease.' I am seeing this problem in small children now, not because they are drinking alcohol...they are drinking massive amounts of juice! If you imagine our traditional culture, fruit is a seasonal summer food when we were most active. We didn't have semi trucks shipping in oranges from other countries to a factory squeezing all the fructose out to form a sweet drink. Eating an orange is fine, but drinking 6 of them in a 8 ounce glass is too hard on our children's liver. Different types of fruit have different levels of fructose too. Rhubarb is very low in fructose, where tropical fruits like bananas are very high.

Here is an interesting fact... Welch's 100% grape juice (NO SUGAR ADDED...just grape juice) has more sugar/fructose in 8 ounces than a 12 ounce can of Mountain Dew! Fructose also has no effect on our hormone Leptin, which tells us to stop eating AND interferes with Ghrelin, which is our hunger hormone.

NUTRITIONAL COMPARISON (per cup)
Rhubarb = 26 calories, 5.5 carbs, 2.2 g fiber (1.3 grams of fructose)
Banana = 200 calories, 51 carbs, 6 g fiber (28 grams of fructose!!!)

Ingredients:

3/4 c. erythritol

2 tsp stevia glycerite

1 (8 oz) package cream cheese
   or coconut cream

2 eggs

1/2 tsp vanilla extract

1/4 tsp Celtic sea salt

3 c. chopped fresh rhubarb

TOPPING:

1/3 c. erythritol

1 tsp stevia glycerite

1/3 c. crushed almonds

1/4 c. almond flour

1/4 c. vanilla whey/
   egg white protein

1 tsp ground cinnamon

1/4 c. butter or coconut oil,
   softened

Directions: Preheat oven to 375 degrees F (190 degrees C). Beat sweetener, cream cheese, and eggs in a large mixing bowl until smooth. Stir in vanilla and salt. Fold in rhubarb. Pour rhubarb mixture into casserole dish. Bake for 30 minutes in the preheated oven. Meanwhile, combine 1/3 cup erythritol and stevia glycerite, 1/3 cup crushed nuts, almond flour, whey and cinnamon in a small bowl. Cut in butter with fork or pastry blender until mixture resembles coarse crumbs. Set aside. Remove rhubarb mixture from oven. Reduce oven temperature to 350 degrees F (175 degrees C). Sprinkle topping mixture evenly over pie. Return crisp to oven and bake until filling is set and crust and topping are golden brown, about 30 minutes.

Makes 12 servings.

NUTRITIONAL COMPARISON (per serving):
Traditional Crisp = 327 calories, 25g fat, 2g protein, 65.7 carbs, 2g fiber
"Healthified" Crisp = 286 calories, 25g fat, 10g protein, 6.9 carbs, 3.5g fiber

Ingredients:

CAKE:

1 c. coconut flour

2 tsp aluminum free
   baking powder

1 tsp Celtic sea salt

1 TBS ground cinnamon

1 1/4 tsp nutmeg

1 tsp ground ginger

1/2 tsp ground allspice

1/4 tsp ground cloves

3/4 c. coconut oil or
   butter, softened

1 1/2 c. erythritol

1 1/2 tsp stevia glycerite

8 eggs

1 1/2 tsp vanilla extract

1 1/2 c. sour cream

FROSTING:

3 (8 oz) pkg cream cheese
   or coconut cream

3/4 c. coconut oil or butter,
   softened

3 TBS unsweetened
   almond milk

1/4 c. erythritol

1 tsp stevia glycerite

Directions:

Put oven rack in middle position and preheat oven to 350°F. Grease cake pans or line cupcake pan with liners. In a large bowl, mix coconut flour, baking powder, salt, and spices. In another bowl (or food processor), beat together butter and sweetener with an electric mixer at medium-high speed until pale and fluffy, 3 to 5 minutes. Beat in eggs 1 at a time, beating well after each addition, then beat in sour cream and vanilla. Reduce speed to low, then add coconut flour mixture and blend until batter is just smooth. Spoon batter evenly into pans (or cupcake liners) to about 2/3 full. Bake until pale golden and a wooden pick inserted in center of cakes comes out clean, 30 to 35 minutes. Cool 10 minutes in pans on racks. Run a thin knife around edge of pans, then invert racks over pans and reinvert cakes onto racks to cool completely.
(Dairy allergy: see pg. 9)

FROSTING: Make frosting: Beat together cream cheese, butter, and almond milk in a bowl with clean beaters at medium-high speed until fluffy, 1 to 2 minutes. Mix in sweetener and beat at medium-high speed until frosting is smooth.

ASSEMBLE AND FROST CAKE: Halve each cake layer horizontally with a long serrated knife using a gentle sawing motion. Put 1 layer, cut side up, on a cake stand or large plate and spread with about 3/4 cup frosting. Stack remaining cake layers, spreading about 3/4 cup frosting on each layer and ending with top cake layer cut side down. Spread top and side of cake with remaining frosting.

Serves 24.
NUTRITIONAL COMPARISON (per serving)
Traditional Spice Cake = 325 calories, 25g fat, 4.7g protein, 21carbs, 0g fiber
"Healthified" Spice Cake = 297 calories, 28g fat, 5.5g protein, 4.5 carbs, 2g fiber

Pre-Biotics and Just Like Sugar

If you read labels you might see ingredients like oligofructose and inulin starting to show up on food packages. These 2 words are called 'prebiotics' in the nutrition world. Prebiotics are non-digestible foods that make their way through our digestive system and help good bacteria grow and flourish. Prebiotics keep beneficial bacteria healthy. They are found in small amounts in many plants. Plants with large amounts of oligosaccharides include chicory root. About 90% makes it past digestion in the small intestine and reaches the colon where it performs a different function: that of a prebiotic. Like Sugar contains 96 grams of inulin fiber per cup! The ingredients of Just Like Sugar = Chicory Root, Calcium and Vitamin C.

Prebiotics help increase probiotics, which are beneficial bacteria that help keep your digestive system healthy. The majority of my clients have malfunctioning digestive systems for a variety of reasons. Our typical 'Western' eating habits and stress can all negatively impact the 'good bacteria' in our gut. Probiotics are helpful micro-organisms that live in our intestinal tract. In a healthy body, good bacteria make up most of the intestines' micro-flora and protect digestive health. If you have primarily good bacteria, your immune system will function optimally and it will help you extract essential nutrients in the foods you eat. In order to feed our cells, we need to absorb the nutrients from our food, otherwise our brain will keep telling us to eat until the cells are fed.

Here are the most common warning signs of a bacterial imbalance, if you suffer one or more of these problems it is quite likely that eating prebiotics and taking a probiotic supplement could help you get your 'system' back on the right track:

1. Allergies and food sensitivities
2. Difficulty losing weight, sugar/carbohydrate craving
3. Frequent fatigue, poor concentration
4. Frequent constipation or diarrhea
5. Faulty digestion, acid reflux and other gut disorders
6. Sleeping poorly, night sweats
7. Painful joint inflammation, stiffness
8. Bad breath, gum disease and dental problems
9. Frequent colds, flu or infections
10. Chronic yeast problems
11. Acne, eczema skin and foot fungus
12. Extreme menstrual or menopausal symptoms

There are many stresses and factors that can kill your 'friendly bacteria' every day. Here is a summary of some of the commonest good-bacteria-KILLERS:

1. Antibiotics
2. Birth control pills
3. Steroidal & hormonal drugs
4. Fluoride (added to toothpaste and sometimes to drinking water!)
5. Chlorine (added to water to kill bacteria...it kills friendly-bacteria too!)
6. Coffee/Tea
7. Carbonated drinks
8. Stress
9. Preservatives
10. Additives (colorings, flavorings and chemicals in processed foods)
11. Pesticides (choose ORGANIC fruit and veggies to avoid this!)
12. Fertilizers (choose ORGANIC fruit and veggies to avoid this!)

Our moods are directly correlated to the intestinal flora of our gut...the nervous system actually come from the gut to the brain; in the past scientists thought the nervous system ran the other way. This is why what we put in our stomach is so essential to our mental health. Having healthy intestinal flora; which you can achieve with probiotics and fermented foods, increase our moods and decrease our cravings. To read more on Probiotics and Cravings, check out my book Secrets to Controlling Your Weight Cravings and Mood.

Ingredients:

- 1/2 c. butter/coconut oil
- 3/4 c. erythritol
- 2 tsp stevia glycerite
- 1 c. Just Like Sugar
- 2 eggs
- 1 c. unsweetened cocoa powder
- 1 tsp Celtic sea salt
- 2 tsp vanilla

Directions:

Preheat the oven to 350 degrees F. In a medium bowl, cream the butter, erythritol, stevia and the Just Like Sugar together. Add in the eggs, stir until well combined. Finally mix in the cocoa powder, salt and vanilla. Form 2 inch balls. Place on a cookie sheet about 2 inches apart. Bake for 10 minutes. Allow to cool on the cookie sheet before removing.

Makes 12 cookies.

NUTRITIONAL COMPARISON (per cookie)

Traditional Cookie = 151 calories, 9g fat, 1g protein, 21 carbs, 2g fiber

"Healthified" Cookie = 92 calories, 9g fat, 2g protein, 6.5 carbs, 4.6g fiber
(1.9 effective carbs)

VARIATION: Smoosh my "healthified" ice cream recipe in between!

Mocha Fudge Cake

Ingredients:

1 1/2 c. Just Like Brown Sugar

4 TBS butter or coconut oil

6 eggs (OR 3 eggs if using almond flour)

3 oz unsweetened chocolate, melted

3/4 c. sour cream/coconut cream

3/4 c. coconut flour (OR 1 1/2 cup almond flour)

1 1/2 tsp baking soda

3/4 c. hot coffee

1 1/2 tsp vanilla or chocolate extract

1/2 tsp Celtic sea salt

Directions:

Pre-heat oven to 350°. Beat Just Like Sugar and butter in a bowl until combined. Beat in eggs, then chocolate, then sour cream. Sift the coconut/almond flour and baking soda in a bowl; add to chocolate mixture. Beat in coffee, vanilla and salt until combined. Coat a 9" cake pan with coconut oil spray; next, pour in batter. Bake until a toothpick inserted in center comes out clean, 35 minutes.

Makes 12 servings.
NUTRITIONAL COMPARISON (per serving)

Traditional Cake =
279 calories, 11g fat, 4g protein, 42 carbs, 2g fiber

"Healthified" Almond Cake =
200 calories, 18g fat, 6g protein, 5.8 carbs, 2.7g fiber

"Healthified" Coconut Cake =
162 calories, 11g fat, 6g protein, 11 carbs, 7g fiber

Lava Cake & Coffee Ice Cream

Ingredients:

CAKE:

8 tsp plus 1/2 cup erythritol

1 tsp stevia glycerite

4 oz unsweetened chocolate, chopped

3/4 c. butter/coconut oil

3 large eggs

3 large egg yolks

1/4 c. unsweetened almond milk

COFFEE ICE CREAM:

5 egg yolks

3/4 c. Just Like Sugar

1/4 c. erythritol

1 tsp stevia glycerite

1 c. heavy whipping cream or coconut cream

1 c. unsweetnened almond milk

1 1/2 c. whole coffee beans (decaf and organic)

1 tsp Celtic sea salt

Directions...

CAKE: Grease 8 (3/4-cup) soufflé dishes or custard cups. Sprinkle inside of each dish with 1 teaspoon sweetener. In a medium saucepan, stir chocolate and butter over low heat until smooth. from heat. Using electric mixer, beat eggs, egg yolks, almond milk and remaining 1/2 cup sweetener in large bowl until thick and pale yellow, about 8 minutes. Fold 1/3 of warm chocolate mixture into egg mixture, then fold in remaining chocolate. Divide batter among soufflé dishes. NOTE: This can be made a few days ahead. Cover with plastic; chill. Bring to room temperature before baking. Preheat oven to 400°F. Place soufflé dishes on a baking sheet. Bake cakes uncovered until edges are puffed and slightly cracked but center 1 inch of each moves slightly when dishes are shaken gently, about 8-9 minutes (still a little gooey in the middle). Top each cake with scoop of coffee ice cream; serve immediately.

Makes 8 servings.
NUTRITIONAL COMPARISON (per serving)
Traditional Molten Cake = calories, 28g fat, 5.4g protein, 24 carbs, 3.5g fiber
"Healthified" Cake = 272 calories, 28g fat, 5.4g protein, 4.7 carbs, 2.4g fiber

COFFEE ICE CREAM: Heat the almond milk, sweeteners, whole coffee beans, salt, and 1/2 cup of the cream in a medium saucepan until it is very warm, but not boiling. Once it is warm, remove from the heat and let steep at room temperature for 1 hour. In a medium saucepan place the egg yolks and sweeteners in to mix on high with a hand mixer. Whip yolks until light in color and double in size. Stir in the rest of the whipping cream. Place the saucepan onto medium heat on the stove and cook, stirring constantly. Stir until thickened into a custard. Remove from heat and stir in the almond milk coffee mixture. Let cool completely (I cooled overnight...it was hard to wait!). Place into your ice cream machine and watch the magic happen within 45 minutes or according to your ice cream maker's directions. Freeze until set.

Makes 5 servings.
NUTRITIONAL COMPARISON (per 1/2 cup serving)
Ben & Jerry's Ice Cream = 230 calories, 15g fat, 4g protein, 23 carbs, 0g fiber
"Healthified" Ice Cream = 137 calories, 13g fat, 3.4g protein, 1.3 carbs, 0g fiber,

Alopecia and Food Allergies

Do you or someone you know suffer from an auto immune disease? My client, who suffers from alopecia (auto immune disease where you lose all your hair) had no hair when I first met her. Well, she showed up today with a surprise! She took her hat off for me and "TADA!" She thought I was crazy when I told her that she had a food allergy causing her to lose her hair. She is a total believer now! She was so excited that she had her first hair cut in over 10 years!

There are two types of allergic reactions:

1. Type A (classic allergy). In this type of allergy, you experience a reaction immediately after contact with an allergen; such as shellfish or peanuts, and can cause swelling in the throat or more serious reactions.
2. Type B (delayed allergy or intolerance). The reactions from type B can take place one hour to 3 days after eating the food. Symptoms are weight gain, bloating, water retention, depression, fatigue, aching joints and headaches.

The phenomenon of allergies and addictions to both foods and chemicals is now well established by doctors specializing in the diagnosis and treatment of allergies. These doctors believe that many chronic health problems, such as migraines, fatigue, mood disorders, and arthritis are often caused by allergies to foods and involve around one-third of the people living in America. Food sensitivities and allergies have a huge effect on the portion of the brain that controls our emotions, memory and body functions, such as body temperature, hunger, thirst, sleep and blood pressure. It has recently been proven that 85 percent of migraine sufferers could be symptom-free when they followed a diet excluding the ten most common food allergens. The most problem-some allergens were cigarettes, coffee, and birth control pills. The studies also found that these allergens caused arthritis, asthma and diabetes.

Be aware that the same food can cause different reactions in people. A person's genetic disposition to allergies will determine which part of the body will become the vulnerable target. Any major organ may be affected: the symptoms of cerebral allergies are hyperactivity, ADHD, depression, irritability, headaches and some forms of schizophrenia; hypoglycemia is a sign of pancreatic malfunction.

Chocolate Cake

Ingredients:

1 1/4 c. erythritol
1 tsp stevia glycerite
1 3/4 c. peanut flour
3/4 c. unsweetened
   cocoa powder
1 1/2 tsp baking soda
1 1/2 tsp baking powder
1 tsp Celtic sea salt
2 eggs
1 c. unsweetened
   almond milk
1/2 c. butter or
   coconut oil
2 tsp vanilla extract

FROSTING:

3/4 c. butter/coconut oil
3 oz cream cheese/coconut cream
1 1/2 c. unsweetened
   cocoa powder
2 c. Just Like Sugar
   (or powdered erythritol)
1 tsp stevia glycerite
3/4 c. unsweetened
   almond milk
1 teaspoon vanilla extract

Directions:

Preheat oven to 350 degrees F (175 degrees C). Grease two 9 inch cake pans. In a medium bowl, stir together the sweetener, peanut flour, cocoa, baking soda, baking powder and salt. Add the eggs, almond milk, oil and vanilla, mix for 3 minutes with an electric mixer. Pour evenly into the two prepared pans. Bake for 30 to 35 minutes in the preheated oven, until a toothpick inserted comes out clean. Cool for 10 minutes before removing from pans to cool completely. To make the frosting, use the second set of ingredients. Cream butter and cream cheese until light and fluffy. Stir in the cocoa and sweetener alternately with the milk and vanilla. Beat to a spreading consistency. Split the layers of cooled cake horizontally, cover the top of each layer with frosting, then stack them onto a serving plate. Frost the outside of the cake. (See page 120 for Frosting)

Serves 12.
NUTRITIONAL COMPARISON (per serving):

Using white flour, skim milk and sugar =
655 calories, 25g fat, 7g protein, 111 carbs, 5.8 fiber

Using peanut flour, almond milk and Just Like Sugar =
314 calories, 25g fat, 9.5g protein, 13.8 carbs, 7.1 fiber

Recipe Index

Recipes in Alphabetical Order